FRom

The Art of Peaceful Living

The Art of
Peaceful Living

Acharya Ramesh Kaushal
(Astrologer & Reiki Grand Master)

NEW DAWN PRESS, INC.
USA • UK • INDIA

NEW DAWN PRESS GROUP
Published by New Dawn Press Group
New Dawn Press, Inc., 244 South Randall Rd # 90, Elgin, IL 60123
e-mail: sales@newdawnpress.com

New Dawn Press, 2 Tintern Close, Slough, Berkshire, SL1-2TB, UK
e-mail: salesuk@newdawnpress.org

New Dawn Press (An Imprint of Sterling Publishers (P) Ltd)
A-59, Okhla Industrial Area, Phase-II, New Delhi-110020, India
e-mail: info@sterlingpublishers.com
www.sterlingpublishers.com

The Art of Peaceful Living
Copyright © 2005, Sterling Publishers (P) Ltd.
ISBN 1-84557-517-2
Reprint 2006, 2007

All rights are reserved. No part of this publication may be reproduced, stored in a retrieval system or transmitted, in any form or by any means, mechanical, photocopying, recording or otherwise, without prior written permission of the publisher.

PRINTED IN INDIA

Dedicated

to

SAI ASTRO-REIKI
RESEARCH FOUNDATION

Acknowledgements

I would like to express my love and blessings to dear little daughter Alpana who helped and supported me in writing this book till its completion. The patience and tolerance of my wife Asha & son Karan is also praiseworthy.

Thanks are indebted to Pandit Naresh Chandra, an incredible expert co-astrologer, who has contributed a lot by inspiring and giving innumerable suggestions.

I would also like to express my gratitude to Dhir sisters our family friends and unconditional well-wishers for their help.

I would like to express my deep debt and gratitude to my learned friend Mr Kamal Kataria and Mr S S Rathore who supported me with their literary knowledge and also helped in editing the book.

I fail in my duties if I do not remember Dr B M Palan, MD, D Clin Hypno (USA) who headed the Psychosomatic Medicine & Hypnotherapy Clinic, SSG Hospital Badodara. His guidance in hypnosis and sweet & soothing voice has always been an inspiring instrument to me.

I whole heartedly thank my Reiki Guru Dr N K Sharma & Dr Savita Sharma of Reiki Healing Foundation, New Delhi for always keeping their hands of blessings on me.

By the Almighty's blessings my inner conscious persuaded me to touch the reality of life and be one with the book.

Preface

It was one of the astrology seminars held at Vrindaban in September 2002, which inspired me to write something on peaceful living. Many of the speakers expressed their views and thoughts on astrology and other 'divine' subjects, but I felt that they all knew about astrology but most of them were expressing their views under stress, for one reason or the other. This very reflection stimulated me to write on handling the stress.

My pilot co-astrologer, Pandit Naresh Chandra, in his speech, emphasised that the astrology community should also be equipped with the knowledge of handling stress to benefit the society. His very idea inspired me to write something on 'Stress and Meditation'.

It was my subject as I have been doing 'Vipassana Meditation' regularly for the last so many years and also knew so many other techniques on meditation. My keen interest to read the books, magazines and articles on occult sciences and related subjects such as William Hart's *Art of Living* on 'Vipassana Meditation', Dayanand Verma's *Dhyan Yog* and Dr Deepak Chopra's hand book on human body- *Ageless Body and Timeless Mind* inspired me in this regard.

The globalisation and advancement in the surrounding environment has paved the way for many complicated demands and expectations, which is the major source of stress. A series of research has proved that stress at the workplace is increasing and unable to cope up, which leads to many physical and mental problems.

But all stresses are not bad. Some people thrive under stressful conditions whereas some rise to top by managing it. But most of the times stress overpowers the person, which leads to many problems. A decade before it was thought to overcome the stress through the management of stress, but at present it is a part and parcel of our lives and the environment we live in.

Most of the time you don't know exactly what is happening inside your body until something goes wrong. Consequently, unchecked ignorance becomes dangerous. For decades, doctors have been warning that stress is the cause of deteriorating health.

There are a number of reliable and effective techniques, which can help a person to cope up with stress and manage it effectively. This improves resulting in positive & optimistic thinking, self-confidence, motivation, high morale, self-expression and overall personality development. This book is a practical guide to the human body and mind describing potentials of physical and emotional development and getting success through many techniques.

The main aim of this book is to describe how inner conscious influences materialistic body. It guides how one can get a successful, happy and peaceful life keeping oneself away from stress. It is basically designed to stimulate the ability to realise stress, and control it before it overpowers. A complete reading of this book will enrich you with a vast knowledge of your inner awakening and learning number of techniques on meditation and self-awareness.

You will understand and recognise the conditions evolving stress, its concept, and types of stress related to physical and emotional symptoms. It will enable you to handle the stress effectively by learning various techniques used like nutrition, time management, affirmations, hypnosis, role and benefits of meditation etc.

Today, stress is something that we accept, we have learnt to live and die with it. This book will help you to know how to come out of stress habits so that life becomes better. You will soon discover that stress management is very normal but very important and indispensable part of life. This will bring significant healthy changes in you, which will reflect upon your personal as well as professional life positively.

I feel myself proud of being a president of a well-established non-profitable registered society *"Sai Astro-Reiki Research Foundation"*. One of the main objectives of this society is to promote astrology and Reiki education for the overall development of modern society and to keep general public aware of unnecessary myths of astrology.

The funds of this society are generated in the form of membership, donations, organising astrology & Reiki classes/consultations etc., to implement the programmes and activities enumerated in the objectives. This book is another step ahead for generating funds for the society. So the income generated through publication will be utilised in the form of donations for the development of this society.

Last but not the least; I hope the present book will be able to meet your requirements. Your valuable suggestions will help me in improving the subsequent editions. I hope my attempt will help the busy persons too.

Acharya Ramesh Kaushal
(Astrologer & Reiki Grand Master)

C-140, Eastend Apptts,
Mayur Vihar Ph-I (Extn),
Delhi-1110 096
Cell: 9810130291
e-mail: siaastro@sify.com

Contents

	Acknowledgement	vi
	Preface	vii
1.	What is Stress	1
2.	How to Cope with Stress	8
3.	Techniques to Reduce Stress	13
4.	Time Management	33
5.	Affirmations	36
6.	Hypnosis	43
7.	Meditation	63

MEDITATION TECHNIQUES

8.	Vipassana Meditation	76
9.	Chakra Recitation	81
10.	Mantra Recitation	85
11.	Pollution Free Meditation	89
12.	Tranquil Meditation (*Trataka*)	91
13.	Energy Healing Meditation	93
14.	Ascension Meditation	94

1
What is Stress?

Stress is the 'wear and tear' conditioning of the body, which reflects physical and emotional effects altogether. It normally happens when you are worried or uncomfortable about something, leading to many disorders in your body like feeling angry, frustrated, scared or afraid and feel irritable.

Most of the people feel that aspects of their work and lifestyle causes stress which is true to some extent, but there are several other major sources of stress such as environment, food and other factors. Adverse pressures at work or in social situations can also cause stress.

It is often observed that some adjustments are needed when there is a physical, psychosocial or material change in our environment, which we could not even recognise as damaging or harmful. The way our body and mind respond to the need for adjustment is called stress. Assumptions of stress are considered to be both, a tense physical as well as mental condition.

Stress is the way one responds to the present changed conditions physically, mentally and emotionally which is sometimes challenging, but seems difficult to tackle. It is a fact that all humans suffer from stress, which is very difficult to ignore.

Stress itself is further one of the principal causes to loss of productivity, social breakdown and ill health. It has been established that most illnesses are related to unrelieved stress. So if you are experiencing stress symptoms, you need to reduce it and improve your ability to manage.

In psychological and technological terms, there are now many possible techniques available to assess accurately and identify the levels of stress in an individual. To measure the areas of weaknesses in individuals and assist them to implement solutions to the problem of stress is possible.

The learning of techniques of stress management is to keep you at a level of stimulation leading to a state of healthy and enjoyable life. These techniques are the effective tools and time tested to reduce or even eliminate sources of unpleasant stress. Before going into the details of these techniques, the types of stressors etc., are needed to be identified so that they are tackled with their respective areas of improvement. These techniques are explained in detail in the forthcoming chapters.

Optimum Stress

Stress is essential for life, but everyone has unique tolerance power to handle it upto some extent. Some people can handle the big stressful events better than the little daily stresses, whereas few others are the opposite. In other words, whatever triggers stress is different for everyone, but no matter how bad things get, it is possible to cope with every stressful event on day-to-day basis. Moderate degree of stress prepares us to meet with the reactions of our body and mind more efficiently. For example:

Stress and Sitar

- Think of a sitar. If its strings are loose, it will produce boring music. So without stress, there would be no charm in life.
- If strings are very tight, the music will be awful and strings will break. Hard stress is dangerous in the same way.
- If strings are optimally tight, you get melodious music. So by stressing ourselves to the optimum level, you can achieve success and satisfaction in life.

Holding stress is like holding weight continuously

- If you hold a very light object in your hand for a longer time, it does not matter; it makes no strain on you.
- It depends how long you can hold it. If you hold it for a minute, it is good, if for an hour, you will have an ache in your arm.
- You will face trouble if you continue to hold it for a day.
- It is exactly the same weight, the longer you hold it, the heavier it becomes. If you carry your burdens all the time, sooner or later, you will not be able to carry as it becomes increasingly heavier.
- What you have to do is to put the weight down, rest for a while before holding it up again. You have to put down the burden periodically, so that you can be refreshed and are able to carry it again.

- When you return home from work, put the burden of work down. Don't carry it home.

To make the life more enjoyable we all need challenges that we can cope with. Sadly, we are at times, faced with challenges that we feel we cannot cope with resulting in stress. Every successful handling of the demand adds to our resources and coping abilities. This is the process of self-development.

Types of Stress

Different individuals have different stressors. The very awareness of the stressor eliminates half of the stress. Therefore, the first step in learning to control stress is to find out the stressors. Some of the common stressors are as under:

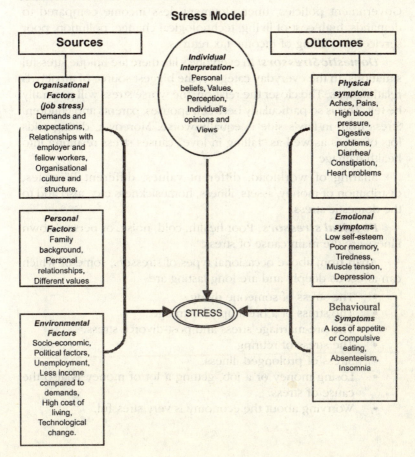

High stress prone professions: Security personnel, police, doctors, emergency workers, staff working under any minister, other time-bound operations are obviously stressful jobs.

Ordinary high stress work: Almost all the occupations come under this category. It doesn't matter if you're an employee, taxi driver, student or businessman. All the work fields have some percentage of stress. Though people think that most of the jobs are not stressful, but actually they are.

Career related stressors: Career consciousness, examination, interview, public speaking, settling of business, training at work place, poor communication, ill-defined role, competition, power struggle etc., are career related stressors.

Socio-economic, political and environmental stressors: Government policies, unemployment, less income compared to demands, high cost of living, technological change, pollution, poor services and filling of income tax returns.

Domestic Stressors: In everyone's life there are unique stressful situations. In the everyday category, the biggest source of anxiety is relationships. The closer the relation, the worse stress will generally be felt. This is so particularly between spouses, parents and children. Stress from in-law's side is equally worse. Moreover, dating adds lots of stress as well as "falling in love" causes stress resulting into health damage.

Sharing of workload, different values, different lifestyles, distribution of money/assets, illness, homesickness etc., also add to the domestic stress.

Physical stressors: Poor health, cold, noise, or person's own illness are the main cause of stress.

Apart from above occasional types of stressors, some of which can affect us deeply and are long lasting are:

- The stress of someone dying.
- The stress of a breakup of marriage.
- The pre-marriage stress and post-divorce stress.
- The stress of retiring.
- Stress of prolonged illness.
- Losing money or a job, getting a lot of money is also the cause of stress.
- Worrying about the economy is very stressful.

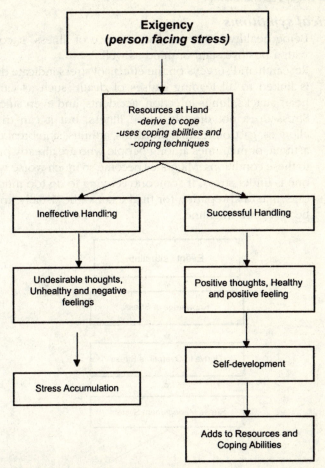

Outcomes/Signs and Symptoms

Before discussing ways to manage stress, it is very important to know what typical signs and symptoms are, when experiencing high levels of stress. Exposure to excessive or repeated stress would cause several negative effects on the person. On some people effects will be visible immediately, whereas on others these will gradually appear as and when the stress is accumulated.

There are two kinds of disease, physical and mental. There are people who enjoy freedom from physical disease for a longer period. But rare ones are those who enjoy freedom from mental disease even for a moment except those who are free from mental defilements.

6   The Art of Peaceful Living

Physical symptoms

- Being healthy is not just the absence of illness. It comes with a positive state of mind as well.
- Research and surveys on the effects of stress indicate that it is linked to all leading causes of death, such as cancer, heart attacks, lungs infection, accidents, and even suicide.
- Stress does not directly cause illness, but it can trigger allergies, gastrointestinal problems, arthritis, skin breakouts, asthma, or migraines among people who are already prone to these conditions. Migraines become so much worse when one is under stress. If someone is trying to do too much at one time (as preparing for final exams), he usually knows he will get a migraine.

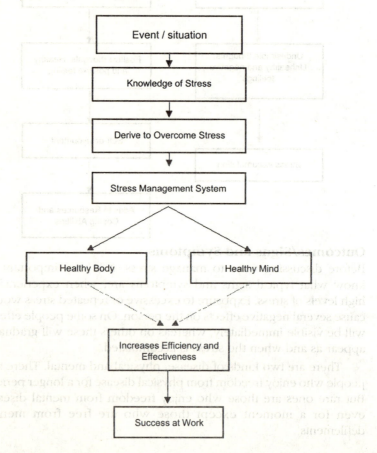

- Higher number of visits to primary care physicians for stress also relates disorders/complaints.
- Mostly the adults suffer adverse health problems due to stress.
- High stress includes—aches, pains, a loss of appetite or compulsive eating, digestive problems, stammering or speaking too fast, grinding teeth during sleep and a reduced sex-desire.

Emotional symptoms

- Unchecked stress can be the root of destroying relationships, losing jobs/promotions and killing someone. Indirectly, stress is one of the biggest killers around us which needs immediate handling.
- Other results of stress can be insomnia, hypertension (high blood pressure), depression and anxiety, smoking, weight gain or weight loss, alcoholism and other substance abuse, immune system problems and resultant infections, mood swings and skin problems etc.
- Tiredness due to muscle tension.
- Poor memory resulting in lack of concentration.
- Changes in sleeping and eating patterns.
- Low self-esteem.

2
How to Cope with Stress

Some degree of stress is very common in most of the people; therefore, the goal is not to eliminate stress but to manage the negative aspects. Everyone has a great deal of control over stress and how it can be dealt with, is a matter of concern.

Small amount of stress is inevitable, but stress management is about coping with these small stresses before they become out of control. It is necessary to take precaution when faced with stress for a longer period; otherwise it can seriously spoil your mental and physical health.

In response to daily stresses, one can have physical reactions like increase in blood pressure, change in heart rate, respiration and metabolism. Since everyone is different from another, the real key is your personal tolerance strength level in stressful situations. Stress management, stress reduction and stress relief can prevent many problems. Prevention is always better than cure.

Effective Coping Skills

If you manage stress, instead of stress managing you, a balanced life is possible. Here are some suggestive measurers to manage stress in your everyday life. Keep these tips in your mind; you will lead a stress free life.

Some don'ts

- **Anger is an energy waster:** Be aware not to become angry or upset. Do not allow yourself to waste your energy where it is not required.
- **Evaluate yourself:** Don't underestimate yourself and overestimate the stress. Try to watch the stress so that you can cope with it, rather than something that overpowers you.
- **Don't oversee excellence every time:** We accept that whatsoever we do must be perfect and excellent, but this

perfection, quickness and excellence are sure to build stress. You may not be hundred per cent perfect and excellent. Superman lives in comic books only, they don't exist in real life.
- ***Don't say yes to everything***: Don't try to be a 'yes man'. Don't agree for each and everything by just simply saying 'yes' when in fact you mean 'no'. This may create trouble for you later on.

Some suggestive alerts
- ***Some indicative warning signs***: The sudden feelings of anxiety, extreme tiredness, crying and feeling of cough and cold may be the warning signs for you. So be aware of such signs instead of ignoring. Ignorance may lead you to stress accumulation.
- ***Review the causes of stress***: Do you analyse how much stress is caused by yourself only? Are your expectations about yourself and others realistic? for example—
- Observe your stressful events: Some people feel tired when they are under a little stress. Do you become nervous or physically upset? If so, try to avoid it slowly.
- Drive out the myths of stress: Stress is very common so nothing can be done to eliminate it. In reality you manage or adjust in your life in such a way so that stress does not overwhelm you. Manage stress through effective planning, prioritising and various coping methods.
- Take every situation thoughtfully: Do not ignore or gloss over your problems. Analyse what events make you stressed out and how your body responds to the stress.
- Your next occurrence is a challenge: Watch out what makes you annoyed or angry for very unimportant matters and then practise to let it go.

Your own indoor exercises to cope
- ***Behave like a relaxed person:*** Repeated actions slowly become natural habit. So try to slow down in your talk, walk and in your pace of living. Soon, this contrived slow pace will become more natural and you will become a relaxed person.
- ***Dealing with a stressful situation:*** Recognise the fact that when you tackle the situation, you change your stressors

by avoiding or eliminating them completely. For example, you are in a joint family and a particular food doesn't suits your body and creates stress. Since you cannot avoid this situation, develop the habit of eating it in less quantity and replace it by other one, which suits you.

- **Reduce the exposure to stress:** While studying for long periods, take a short break every hour. This is a very significant way of getting through stressful times. Sometimes it is difficult to focus and get stuff done when studying continuously for a longer period. So it definitely helps if break is taken once in a while.
- **Divide your stress into smaller parts:** The impact of stress is decreased by dividing it into smaller parts when dealing with a big problem. Once a part of the task is complete, pick up another and so on, hence reducing the volume of stress.
- **Create a mantra:** A mantra is a repeated phrase, word, or sentence that reminds you about your goal. It could be something like, 'Smile', 'Relax' and 'Let it go'. Repeat it silently or loudly over and over again while you consciously slow your breathing down and deepen it, till the tension drains out of your face, jaws, neck, and shoulders.
- **Ways to control physical reactions:** Before reacting to the next stressful occurrence, take few deep breaths and release them slowly assuming that you are coming out of tension. Slow and deep breathing will bring your heart and pulse rate back to normal. If you have a little time at your disposal, try out some relaxation techniques such as meditation or yoga.
- **Lay down your priorities:** When life seems to be too complicated, determine what things are really important to you. List them and do it on priority basis. Prepare a list of things, which you would like to do first and then do rest of the things one by one.
- **Every problem has a solution:** There are number of solutions or alternatives to every problem. Always remember you have choices. Stress-free people remain aware of this simple fact. When things seems impossible, say to yourself, "I have a choice".
- **Flexible values of judgements:** Stop judging others by your own values. Don't always measure others up to your

expectations. Everyone has his own values and desires. Don't try to mould them according to your wish or needs. Don't be disappointed or frustrated when this happens and don't waste time in changing the individual. Everyone has his virtues and shortcomings, so be flexible.
- *Laugh:* Laughter is the best medicine. Get together with people who are really cheerful and amusing and let the stress go away from you.
- *Do rehearsals:* Visualise yourself handling a stressful situation very effectively and confidently. Many people feel these "rehearsals" boost self-confidence and give them a positive approach to the task at hand.
- *A pet is a faithful friend:* If you are lonely or socially isolated, a pet can prove to be a very good friend of yours. But sometimes a new pet can create many hassles, which could potentially add to your stress if you are living in a hyper-busy environment.

Your own outdoor exercises to cope
- *Carry out community service:* Your self-esteem and confidence rises when you do something for others. Sometimes you get a different perspective for example, what is important in life or how hard life can treat others. Your problems seem to be manageable, but your help may lead others to come out of miseries. Pick a service or program that has meaning for you as well as for the community and involve yourself fully with it.
- *Enjoy nature:* There is a soothing force in nature, which cannot be expressed in words, but you only experience it. Just spare sometime and get away from busy life for few days or hours. Do visit the mountains, the ocean, the forest, river, field, and a park and enjoy the nature's beauty. So enjoy the nature at least for sometime, completely forgetting everything.
- *Spare sometime for yourself:* Remember the last time you pampered yourself in a long hot bath, a massage, a new haircut, a small shopping spree, a vacation, quiet time alone? This would give you more relief, mentally and physically.
- *Identify someone who really listens to you:* You have a volume of thoughts to share, but no one has time to listen

to you. Most of the times you don't need advice, you just need someone to listen to you patiently and try to understand what circumstances you are going through. This makes you feel lighter and at ease many times.

- ***Plenty of outside resources are available:*** There are many books, tapes and videos available in libraries, book stores and also in stress management centres. You are to decide according to your resources, time at your disposal and according to your taste, what appeals to you the most.
- ***Do something to relax:*** You may be at your workplace or on the roadside while driving, feel free to include a period of relaxation every day.
- ***Attend relaxation techniques:*** You may attend a workshop or buy a tape and start practising relaxation. You will be able to relax yourself fully and let the stress go.
- ***Physical exercise:*** Even a ten-minute walk can help to clear your head, change your perspective or raise your energy level. If you are stressed, this type of activity can really diversify your attention to another direction and can do physiological and psychological wonders.
- ***Select an outside interest or hobby:*** It is important to have something in your life that is non-competitive and constructive like gardening, photography, wood-working and so on. There should be something to enjoy which helps you to feel peaceful and at ease.
- ***Attend a yoga class or meditation workshop:*** Open your mind to other possible ways of viewing the world. Yoga and meditation will have a drastic positive effect on your body and mind.
- ***Stress management training course:*** Make a schedule to attend a stress management training course, even if you are not under stress. This will add to your vocabulary of coping stress if required. But on the other hand you do not have to be stressed to attend one of these immediately.

3
Techniques to Reduce Stress

There are number of worldwide effective techniques suggested and worked out by various experts, but following are the most commonly used techniques for stress reduction:
- **Nutrition**
- **Time management**
- **Affirmations**
- **Hypnosis**
- **Meditation**

Nutrition
Life is a continuous process, and good health makes it smooth and fast. Unhygienic and unbalanced diet will surely have adverse effect on body as well as mind. Nutritious and hygienic diet keeps the body in perfect condition and helps to face stress efficiently.

The following nutritious tips will help you achieve your health goal. However the correct diet is proportional to the structure of your body and can be well advised by the dietician. According to most diet experts, the best diet is a low-cholesterol, rich in vitamins and minerals and moderate in protein.

The following suggestions are recommended for well-balanced and nutritious meals:
- *Eat a balanced diet:* Consuming nutritious or hygienic food alone does not serve the purpose. The food we consume should be balanced. Sometimes we are down with stress due to improper food/non-eating habits. The carbohydrates do not make the person fat until and unless they are eaten in bulk. So you need a nutritious diet rich in vitamins, minerals and fiber like vegetables, fruits, potatoes, whole wheat bread, pasta, rice, oats, beans, soya and whole grain cereals etc.
- *The rich food:* It is suggested to take rice, dry chapattis, pulses, diluted (without cream) milk, vegetables, fruits,

fibrous items, buttermilk and salad etc., for maintaining good health. Eat complex carbohydrates such as whole meal bread, jacket potatoes etc. Vegetables in particular contain a range of enzymes and other micronutrients that are essential for an efficient metabolism. So the intake of vegetables should be more in daily diet.

- *Take proteins and fats earlier in the day:* A high protein diet keeps blood sugar levels stable and may also lead to average weight loss at the initial stage. So to digest proteins quickly the body needs the later hours of the day and during sleep to detoxify itself.

  If we eat food late and especially which are digested slowly, our metabolism works for digestion only rather than purifying our system from the waste by-products of eating.

- *Drink plenty of water:* Water is one of the keys to balance our bodies. Drink plenty of water, at least 10-15 glasses a day, which will help you to dehydrate your body. In order to keep away the side effects of caffeine, tea and diuretic medicines, you are advised to take more water. Drinking of water should be avoided with the meals and should be consumed between the intervals of meals.

- *Intake of sugar and salt to a minimum:* The intake of sugar and salt to a minimum can help you to support your immune system as it fights against colds and flu.

- *Avoid these:* One must avoid oily and non-vegetarian food, stale and spicy food, soft drinks and concentrated milk, ice creams, nicotine, excessive caffeine and other stimulants.

- *Over-consumption of food:* Candy, chocolate, cookies, biscuits, sweets, cakes etc., are all high in refined carbohydrates and will lead to weight gain.

- *Avoid acidic diet:* A too acidic diet leads to breakdown of vital organs and functions inside the body. To keep balance in diet in respect of acidity and alkalinity, eat 80% alkaline and 20% acidic diet. The way to achieve this is, eating more fresh fruits and vegetables, while reducing animal meats and processed sugar products.

- **Intelligent combination of food:** The appropriate timing and combination of intake of food is necessary. Acidic combinations include eating vegetables with fruits or fruits along with starch products like bread. Eat fruits separately whenever possible.

- ***Eat vegetarian food:*** Health conscious people in India and even in Western countries have started adopting pure vegetarian food. The vegetarian food contains:
  - Nutrients like iron – cashews, tomato juice, rice, and lentils.
  - Calcium in dairy products, fortified soya milk and fortified orange juice.
  - Vitamin D – in fortified and soya milk, and prepared cereals or a small amount of sunlight.
  - Vitamin B12 – dairy products and fortified soya milk, cereals and products made from soya beans (they are low in calories and rich in protein).
  - Zinc – in whole grains (especially the germ and bran of the grain), dairy products, nuts, leafy vegetables, and root vegetables (onions, potatoes, carrots, celery, radishes) and
  - Protein – vegetarians must eat a variety of plant foods in order to get enough protein. Plant foods that have the most protein are lentils, nuts, seeds, and peas etc.

Meal Schedule

Scheduling time for meals is very important. Proper intake of food keeps you energetic throughout the day. It ensures that your digestive system remains healthy and frees you from acidity, ulcers and other systemic functions. This is only possible if you normally do not take fried and spicy foods.

Another major precaution to be taken is that if you are, once in a while, lured to overeat in social gatherings or parties, seeing the sumptuous food, you should necessarily and strictly balance your meals for the next two or three days and also go for extra workouts and exercises.

If you really value your body and watch the eating schedule in a disciplined manner, take it guaranteed that you will prevent unnecessary weight gain and at the same time keep yourself more healthy. Given below is a tentative chart and menu of interval vegetarian eatables:

Breakfast (8 a.m.)

This is the first solid meal for the day. This is the meal being eaten by you after a gap of about 12 hours, so you should never skip this meal. This meal provides you with all the nutrients that your body

requires for the day. Both the quantity and quality of your meal are important. Take the following choices:
- Seasonal fruit/Sprouted pulses

    and
- Corn flakes + 200 ml milk/coffee/150 ml fruit juice or Dalia

    and
- White bread (2 slices) with 10 gm butter/40 gm cottage cheese/Small plain dosa/2 pieces idly

Midmorning tea/snacks (10.30 a.m.)

During your work place or at home you need interval meals before Lunch. Following options are better:
- Buttermilk/ fruit juice/ vegetable juice/tea or coffee with 1-2 biscuits.

Lunch (1.30 p.m.)

This meal replenishes the energy you have spent in the morning. It is important that this meal is balanced and nutritive.
- Veg Soup (150-200 ml)
- Vegetable salad (1 serving of 100 gms)
- Any dal
- Seasonal dry vegetable
- Two pieces of chapatti (60 gms)/rice (150 gms)
- Curd (1 bowl)

Tea time (4.30 p.m.)

Have a beverage or a little fruit.
- Tea/Coffee (preferably without milk and sugar) with 1-2 biscuits

Dinner (8.00 p.m.)

Dinner also needs to be lighter, nutritive and balanced. Do not skip this meal. It keeps your system ticking for the next twelve hours or so. Do not have dinner later than 8.30 p.m. and sorry, no alcohols recommended. Enjoy with following menu:
- Tomato Soup/Rasam
- Mixed Salad
- Dry Vegetable
- Dal (whole or broken) or vegetable with gravy
- Fried rice (150 gms)/Khichadi (150 gms)/Vegetable Pulao (100 gms) **or** 2 Chapattis (Fried rice, pulao and greasy preparations should be occasional)

- One piece sweet.

Although it may seem a little out of place, but brushing your teeth after every solid meal to keep away the deposits in gum cavities, is a very important tool for maintaining a good health.

Nutritive Value of Some Common Food Stuffs

Having discussed the regularisation of meal habits, it is very important to gain knowledge of nutritive values of some common eatables so that you are more cautious to choose the right food at the right time.

Body needs a wide range of nutrients to perform various functions and to lead a healthy life. These nutrients include proteins, fats, carbohydrates, vitamins and minerals. These are the chemical substances which are present in the food we eat daily.

Depending on the relative concentration of these nutrients, food is classified as *protein rich food, carbohydrate rich food and fat rich food* etc. Some foods provide only a single nutrient as in the case of sugar, which is only a source of carbohydrates while oil, ghee etc., provide only fats.

While vitamins and minerals do not supply energy, they play a very important role in the regulation of the metabolic activity in the body.

We need all the above nutrients i.e., energy, protein, vitamins, minerals in different amounts to grow, live and thrive. Since man derives all the nutrients he needs through the diet he eats, his diet must be well-balanced to provide all the nutrients in proper proportion.

The role that various nutrients play in the living organism is briefed hereunder. Given below are the types of food that are capable of specific functions. These have to be consumed in specified quantities and at specified intervals.

Proteins

Proteins are the body-building nutrients and are vital to any living organism. They are important constituent of tissue and cells of the body. They form the important component of muscle and other tissues and vital body fluids like blood. The proteins in the form of enzymes and hormones are concerned with a wide range of vital metabolic process in the body. Protein supplies the body-building material and makes good the loss that occurs due to wear and tear.

Proteins are required for foetal development in pregnancy, for growth in infant and children and for maintenance in adults. The actual amount of protein to be consumed daily to meet the above requirement will depend upon the quality of dietary protein. The higher the quality, lower the requirement and viceversa.

All foods except refined sugar, oil and fats contain protein to varying degree. Some foods contain a high amount of protein and can be classed as protein rich food like meat, animal foods, fish and egg etc.

Sources
- The body building food could be from two sources – plant/vegetable foods and animal foods. They are pulse, lentil and legume; nut and oilseed; milk and milk products. Dried pulses are rich in proteins. Puffed pulses that are consumed as snacks are also very healthy.
- Nuts and oilseeds contain about 18 to 40% proteins.
- Soyabean is high in protein about 40%. They are used as milk substitutes that can be fed to infants.
- Milk is among the most wholesome of foods. One litre of cow's milk provides about 35 gm of protein and 35 gm of fat.

Fats and Carbohydrates

Fats and carbohydrates are energy giving nutrients. Fat is an important component of diet and serves a number of functions in the body. It is a concentrated source of energy.

Fats in the diet can be of two kinds, the visible and invisible fats. The visible fats are those derived from animal fats like butter, ghee which are solid fats and those derived from vegetables/plants fats like groundnut, mustard, coconut, safflower, til are liquid fats.

In addition to the quantity and quality, the mode of consumption of fat also appears to influence elevation of cholesterol in blood.

Carbohydrates are a class of energy yielding substances which include starch, glucose, cane sugar, milk, sugar etc. Grain foods/roots and tubers are largely composed of starch, a complex carbohydrate. Food ingredients like simple sugars namely cane sugar and glucose are pure carbohydrates.

Though they do not contribute to the nutritive value of foods, but the presence of fibre, i.e., roughage in the diet is necessary for the mechanism of digestion and elimination of waste for which they contribute a lot. The contraction of muscular walls of the digestive tract is stimulated by the fibre, thus counteracting the tendency to constipation. Lack of adequate dietary fibre in diets containing refined foods leads to constipation and colon cancer.

In working out a diet schedule, the requirement of protein, fat, vitamins, and minerals should be considered and carbohydrate rich foods can be included in sufficient amounts to meet the energy needs.

Sources
- Energy giving foods are cereals, sugars, roots and tubers, fats and oils and alcohol.
- Cereals are the staple foods of a large majority of the population of the world.
- Sugars are simple and pure carbohydrates that serve mainly as a source of concentrated energy.
- Roots and tubers in general are good sources of carbohydrates alone and form the staple food in some countries.
- Fats and oils provide double the quantity of energy when compared to carbohydrates.
- Alcohol provides greater energy per gram than carbohydrates, but it has to be used with caution and in limited quantities.

Vitamins
Vitamins and minerals are protectors and regulators for the body's organic system. They are organic substances present in small amounts in many foods. They are required for carrying out many vital functions of the body and many of them are involved in the utilisation of the major nutrients like proteins. Although they are needed in small amounts, but they are essential for health and well-being of the body.

There are thirteen complex organic compounds. Some are water soluble like vitamin C, B complex, thiamine (B1), riboflavin (B2) and some are fat soluble such as vitamins A, D, E and K. The characteristics of few of them are explained hereunder:

Vitamin A: It is necessary for clear vision in dim light. Lack of vitamin A thus leads to night blindness. So it is essential for eyesight. Mainly night blindness is associated with vitamin A deficiency. This also adversely affects skin and organ linings. That is why you have ointments with vitamin A for acne and pimples. Vitamin A deficiency is common among children of the poor in the country.

Sources
- It is present in some animal foods like butter and ghee, whole milk and curd, which are some of the richest known natural sources of vitamin A.
- The rich source of vitamin A is leafy vegetables, spinach, amaranth, coriander, drumstick leaves, curry leaves, mint, radish leaves etc.
- Ripe yellow fruits such as mangoes, papaya and tomatoes are also rich in this vitamin.
- Among other vegetables, carrots and yellow pumpkin are good sources.
- It can be said that in general the greener the leafy vegetables, higher the content of vitamin A.

Intake of large amount of vitamin A for prolonged periods can lead to toxic symptoms which include irritability, headache, nausea, and vomiting. These symptoms however subside on stoppage of the intake.

Vitamin B: There are several vitamins of this category, but the common property of B vitamins is that they are essential for the metabolism and proper utilisation of energy, carbohydrates, protein and fats. An important vitamin of this group is thiamine (B1), and then there is B2, B12 also. A deficiency of this vitamin, affects appetite, skin, eyes, lips, blood, and the nervous system.

Sources
- The richest source of thiamine (Vitamin B1) is yeast and the outer layers of cereals like rice, wheat and millets.
- The commonly consumed foods, which contain a high level of B1, are unmilled cereals, pulses and nuts, particularly groundnut.
- Fruits and vegetables.

Vitamin C: Ascorbic acid called vitamin C is a strong reducing agent. It is involved in collagen synthesis, bone and teeth calcification and many other reactions in the body as a reducing agent. It is essential for the gums. Its deficiency causes scurvy, bleeding gums and defective bone growth.

Sources
- Fresh vegetables and fruits, particularly citrus fruits should be used for obtaining enough vitamin C.
- Fresh meat and milk also contain small quantity of this vitamin.
- Sprouted bengal gram is the best source of vitamin C among sprouted grams.
- Expensive fruits like apple are not the rich source of vitamin C, but fresh fruits like orange, grapes, lime etc., contain good amount of it.
- Very cheap fruits like amla and guava are very rich sources of vitamin C. Indeed amla is one of the richest natural sources of this vitamin.

Vitamin D: It is essential for bones and the skeleton system. Lack of this vitamin leads to rickets and osteomalacia, which initially manifests as pain in bones. It usually starts during pregnancy when the demand for calcium is raised. So good supply of vitamin D during pregnancy benefits the mother and helps satisfactory development of the infant. A deficiency of this vitamin in a child causes rickets, bowlegs, pigeon chest and brittle bones that are easily fractured. In adults, osteoporosis (melting of bones) and osteomalacia are major problems.

Sources
- Vegetables and fruits are the protective and regulatory foods that are rich in the numerous vitamins and minerals listed above.
- The best natural source of vitamin D is direct sunrays.

As in the case of vitamin A, intake of excessive amount of vitamin D can also lead to toxic symptoms including irritability, nausea, vomiting, and constipation.

Minerals

Let us take a brief look at the minerals, the body needs. Most growing organisms need or have organic chemicals such as carbon, oxygen, nitrogen, and hydrogen. Apart from these the human body needs approximately another 28 inorganic chemical elements.

The most important minerals that the body needs are calcium, phosphorus, magnesium, sodium, potassium, chloride, and sulphur. The other important trace elements are – iron, zinc, copper, iodine, manganese, chromium, cobalt, molybdenum, selenium, and fluoride etc.

There are many other minor elements like nitrogen, silicon, vanadium, nickel, tin, cadmium, aluminum, arsenic, strontium, barium, boron, and lithium.

Few of the minerals are briefed hereunder for the over all knowledge of a common man:

Calcium

Calcium is an essential element required for several life processes. As the structural component, calcium is required for the formation and maintenance of skeleton and teeth. It is also required for a number of other essential processes like normal contraction of muscle to make limbs move, contraction of heart for its normal function, nervous activity and blood clotting. These functions are carried out by calcium present in the cells. Calcium present in bone helps to maintain the calcium level in plasma in the case of dietary calcium deficiency.

Children need relatively more calcium than adults to meet the requirements of growing bones. Calcium requirements are also increased during pregnancy to meet the needs of growing foetus. Afterwards, a healthy breast fed baby of 3 months receives a large amount of calcium all of which has been drawn from mother's milk.

Sources

Calcium is available in the following:
- The richest source of calcium among animal foods is milk (butter milk, skim milk and cheese).
- It is present in both animal and plant foods.
- The richest source among vegetables sources is green leafy vegetable group.
- Amaranth, fenugreek tapioca and drumstick leaves.
- Most cereals like ragi and grain contain some amount of this element.
- The habit of chewing betel leaves with slaked lime is a practice quite common in India, particularly among the poor, which increases calcium intake. Calcium ingested in this way can be utilised by the body.
- Rice is a poor source of calcium and therefore insufficiency of calcium is one of the main defects of diets largely based on rice.

Phosphorus

Another major element in the body, important next to calcium is phosphorus. Utilisation of calcium is closely linked with that of phosphorus, since most of the calcium phosphate in the body is deposited as calcium phosphate in the bone and the teeth.

Sources
- The richest source of phosphorus in our diets is cereals and pulses.
- Nuts and oilseeds.

Electrolytes and Trace Elements

It is known now that a large number of elements are required in trace amounts for a wide range of functions in the body. Some of the important trace elements of relevance in human nutrition are zinc, copper, selenium, cobalt, fluoride, manganese, chromium, iodine, molybdenum and many more.

Major elements like iron, sodium, potassium, and magnesium are essential as electrolytes to maintain electrolyte balance. A wide range of trace elements are known to be required for cellular function. Major of them are briefed hereunder:

Iron

Iron is an essential element for the formation of haemoglobin of red blood cells. It is essential for generation of blood and plays an important role in the transport of oxygen. Tissues also require iron for various oxidation/reduction reactions. Most of the iron in the body is reutilised. Some of the body iron is also stored in the liver and spleen.

The amount of iron to be absorbed from daily diet is quite small. Although diet rich in iron may be able to meet our daily iron requirement and prevent iron deficiency, but it may not be effective in correcting iron deficiency (anaemia) as indicated by lower level of haemoglobin in the blood. Pregnant woman because of her high iron requirement often suffer from anaemia even on a diet containing normal levels of iron. In such cases supplementation with iron salts may be essential at least during later half of pregnancy.

Sources
- Rich sources of iron are cereals, millets and pulses. Of the cereal, grains and millets, bajra and ragi are very good sources of iron.

- Inclusion in our daily diet about 50g green leafy vegetables, which are rich sources of iron, can meet a fair proportion of iron needs besides other elements.

Zinc

Zinc is essential for growth as well as fast wound healing. Zinc is an important element performing a range of functions in the body as it is a co-factor for a number of enzymes.

Zinc deficiency leads to growth failure and poor development of gonadal function. Zinc intake and zinc absorption is low in diets of poor income groups in India.

Sources

- Zinc is found in a wide variety of foods, Oysters contain more zinc than any other food. Other good food sources include breads, cereals and other grain products like beans, nuts, certain seafood, whole grains, fortified breakfast cereal etc.

Sodium and Potassium

Sodium and Potassium are important constituents of fluids present outside and within the cell. Proper concentration of these electrolytes inside and outside the cell is essential to maintain osmotic balance and keep cells in proper shape.

Sources

- Plant foods are a rich source of potassium. The amount present in a vegetarian diet is probably adequate to meet the daily requirement.
- Sodium is lost in urine and particularly in sweat as sodium chloride. Sodium present in foods is not adequate to meet the requirement. Hence sodium chloride or common salt has to be included in the diet.
- The daily intake of salt in conditions of excessive sweating as in summer is necessary and for those who work in a hot environment, a slightly higher intake may be needed.

Magnesium

Magnesium is present in small concentration in all cells and is required for cellular metabolism. It is also present in bone along with calcium. Magnesium shares many of the properties of calcium so far as absorption and metabolism and tissue distribution are concerned. Magnesium is also implicated to have a role in cardiovascular disease.

Sources
- Cereals, pulses and nuts. Magnesium content of foods is generally much higher than calcium.
- Leafy vegetables are also a good source of magnesium.

Iodine
Iodine is essential for the thyroid gland and helps to prevent a deficiency disorder called goitre (swelling of the thyroid). Goitre is widespread in many parts of the world.

Iodine deficiency is characterised by swelling of thyroid gland in the throat. In the foetal stage it may lead to mental retardation and in later life retardation of the body growth.

The daily requirement of iodine is reported to be 100-150 mg. In an endemic goitre area, there is iodine deficiency in the soil, water and locally grown foods. Besides, certain compounds present in foods, particularly vegetables such as broccoli, brussels sprouts, cabbage, cauliflower, collards, kale, kohlrabi, mustard, rape, rutabaga and turnip interfere with, iodine utilisation and lead to goitre. They are known as goitrogens.

Sources
- One of the well-tested approaches to control iodine deficiency disease is the distribution of iodised salt.
- Avoid eating above mentioned particular vegetables.

Copper
Copper is an essential element for man. It plays an important role in iron absorption. It is also involved in cross-linking of connective tissues, neurotransmission and lipid metabolism. Part of body copper circulates in plasma as ceruloplasmin. Central nervous system disorders may result from copper deficiency with impaired myelination and catecholamine metabolism.

Other trace elements like chromium, molybdenum, fluoride, selenium, cobalt, silicon, arsenic, nickel, and vanadium etc., are also of greater significance in nutritional system in the human body which plays a significant role.

Calorie Value of Foods
After acquiring the basic knowledge about the nutrients required for our body, here is a compact table of these values, which can be derived by a suggestive intake of specific food.

The Art of Peaceful Living

The table gives the energy and nutritive content of some common foods (per 100 grams) that are consumed in India. Soyabeans have the unbeatable combination of high protein, low fat and high energy. The dals are also very nutritive. Cheese and nuts contain high protein but be careful they also have a lot of fat.

Food	Protein	Fat	Carbohydrate	Energy
Almond	20.8	58.9	10.5	655
Amaranthus	3.0	0.3	7.0	43
Amla	0.5	0.1	13.7	58
Apple	0.2	0.5	13.4	59
Banana	1.2	0.3	27.2	116
Bengal gram dal	20.8	5.6	59.8	372
Black gram dal	24.0	1.4	59.6	347
Brinjal	1.4	0.3	4.0	24
Cabbage	1.8	0.1	4.6	27
Carrot	0.9	0.2	10.6	48
Cashew nut	21.2	46.9	22.3	596
Cauliflower	2.6	0.4	4.0	30
Cheese	24.1	25.1	6.3	348
Crab (muscle)	8.9	1.1	3.3	59
Cucumber	0.4	0.1	2.5	13
Dates	2.5	0.4	75.8	317
Drumstick leaves	6.7	1.7	12.0	92
Green gram dal	24.4	1.4	59.9	348
Groundnut	25.3	40.1	26.1	567
Guava	0.9	0.3	11.2	51
Hilsa	21.8	19.4	2.9	273
Ladies finger	1.9	0.2	6.4	35
Mango ripe	0.6	0.4	16.9	74
Methi leaves	4.4	0.9	6.0	49
Milk - buffalo	4.3	8.8	5.0	117
Milk - cow	3.2	4.1	4.4	67
Onion	1.8	0.1	12.6	59
Papaya - ripe	0.6	0.1	7.2	32
Peas	19.7	1.1	56.5	315
Potato	1.6	0.1	22.6	97
Prawn	19.1	1.0	0.8	89

Table Contd...

Table Contd...

Food	Protein	Fat	Carbohydrate	Energy
Ragi	7.3	1	72.0	328
Rice (parboiled)	6.4	0.4	79.0	346
Rice raw	6.8	0.5	78.2	345
Sardine	21.0	1.9	-	101
Shrimp	68.1	8.5	-	349
Soyabean	43.2	19.5	20.9	432
Sweet potato	1.2	0.3	28.2	120
Tomato ripe	0.9	0.2	3.6	20
Water melon	0.2	0.2	3.3	16
Wheat flour	12.1	1.7	69.4	341

Check Your Weight

It is very important to maintain a standard weight according to your height by strictly adhering to scheduled meals, which keeps you more healthy. A specific height of man or women must contain a measured weight approximately. Here is a formula for calculation of your weight according to your height:

Body Mass = Weight in kilograms/(Height in metres)^2

Normal weight according to standard height is given below to check your figure. This weight can fluctuate by 2 Kg considering fully grown up body at the age of 18 for women and 24 for men:

Height (Feet)	Men: Weight (Kgs)	Women: Weight (Kgs)
5'- 0"	-	50.8 - 54.4
5'- 1"	-	51.7 - 55.3
5'- 2"	56.3 - 60.3	53.1 - 56.7
5'- 3"	57.6 - 61.7	54.4 - 58.1
5'- 4"	58.9 - 63.5	56.3 - 59.9
5'- 5"	60.7 - 62.2	57.6 - 61.2
5'- 6"	60.8 - 65.3	58.9 - 63.5
5'- 7"	64.0 - 68.5	60.8 - 65.4
5'- 8"	65.8 - 70.8	62.2 - 66.7
5'- 9"	67.6 - 72.6	64.0 - 68.5
5'-10"	69.4 - 74.4	65.8 - 70.3
5'-11"	71.2 - 76.2	67.1 - 71.1
6'- 0"	73.0 - 78.5	68.5 - 73.9

Observe Your Diet and Cure Diseases

Maintaining dieting schedule is guaranteed key to keep you away from diseases. So keep on simply observing your diet regularly. A diet check is as necessary as security check at high-risk security zone. To avoid unpleasant emergencies, always be alert on checking hazardous stuff out of the way while you eat. Here's how you eat your way back to health.

Hypertension

Hypertension merely means high blood pressure. Generally all hypertension prone people must keep their blood pressure under control with proper medication and follow the right diet.

A hypertensive person must:
- Reduce salt in the usual foods.
- Avoid high sodium foods like pickles, pappads, chips, fried items and processed foods containing mono sodium glutamate.
- Never reach out for the salt sprinkler.
- Never put on excessive weight.
- Eat plenty of fruits and vegetables
- Exercise mildly but regularly.

Heart diseases

In the disorders of the heart and disruptive blood circulatory system, prepare the diet keeping in mind the following rules.
- Reduce the energy value of the diet, if the person is overweight.
- Restrict the sodium intake if edema is present.
- Reduce intake of saturated fats.
- High blood cholesterol is usually associated with increased incidence of coronary diseases. Cholesterol is found only in fats obtained from animal sources such as egg yolks, milk, cheese, cream, butter, shell fish, brain, kidneys etc. So free yourself by avoiding these to control dietary cholesterol.
- Substitute skimmed milk for whole milk.
- Substitute vegetable fats for animal fats.

Liver Disorders

Liver is the largest organ with complex functions like protein metabolism, carbohydrate storage, and detoxification of some poisons, alcohol metabolism and production of bile.

Infective agents like acute infective hepatitis or toxic substances such as chloroform and certain drugs cause liver injury. The condition is marked by increased concentration of bile pigment in blood. This is observed as yellow pigmentation. You guessed it, it is jaundice. Vomiting, nausea and loss of appetite are significant features of this condition.

A person with such symptoms must:
- Take carbohydrates in the form of fruit juices apart from intravenous glucose, if fluids are tolerated.
- Food can be later altered to suit the taste.
- Avoid heavy and spicy food.
- A pure and hygienic cane juice is preferred.

Hepatic Cirrhosis
This is the advanced chronic condition of liver damage resulting from various forms, especially in association with alcoholism.

A patient must:
- Eat a balanced diet adequate in all nutrients.
- Take sufficient quantity of protein.
- Monitor diet on daily basis to maintain a high-protein and high-energy intake.
- Cirrhosis may be associated with accumulation of fluid in peritoneal cavity. In such an event, restrict the salt intake.

Cholecystitis
This is the inflammation of gall bladder, associated with gallstones and accompanied by obesity. This has also two stages:

Acute Cholecystitis
If the person is suffering from acute cholecystitis, remember:
- Drink plenty of water, glucose and fruit drinks.
- Take a low fat diet. (The presence of fat in the duodenum stimulates gall bladder contraction. A low fat diet is appropriate to keep contraction of gall bladder to the minimum during the period of acute inflammation).

Chronic Cholecystitis
In this case, if surgery is not advised, a suitable long-term regimen is required.

For Chronic Cholecystitis –
- One must have a normal fat intake. This helps to counteract stones of the gall bladder, promotes drainage of the biliary

system and helps to prevent formation of gallstones.
- Fats of milk, butter and eggs are usually well-tolerated.
- Avoid vegetables and fruits causing flatulence.

Ulcer

This is tummy trouble. The inner walls of the stomach or the duodenum are broken resulting in inflammation. This painful condition requires careful monitoring of the food ingested. Intake of the wrong food can cause serious aggravation of the problem.

Ulcer patients must:

- Eat high protein food as protein helps in faster healing of the ulcer.
- Eat food in small quantities at small intervals. A heavy stomach can be very uncomfortable.
- Eat food that is soft in texture and taste. Plenty of milk, eggs, soft boiled cereals, porridges, mashed potatoes can be taken with little sugar or salt.
- Avoid green chillies, red chillies and pepper. Keep all types of spices and condiments at bay until complete cure.
- Drink health beverages, many branded varieties of which are available in the market.

Diabetes Mellitus

Insulin secreted by the pancreas in a diabetic person is inadequate to utilise the glucose in the blood. The glucose cannot be converted to energy and this leads to excessive blood sugar levels. This is dangerous as it can lead to serious complications.

The first prescription a doctor gives is a food prescription. Make sure that it is strictly adhered to. In the early stages, there's no need to pop a pill.

Diabetic person must:

- Eat measured quantities of cereal foods.
- Eat at smaller intervals.
- Eat less carbohydrate and fatty foods.
- Avoid pure sugar forms like crystallised sugar, sweets and confectionery.
- Eat plenty of high-fibre foods like vegetables and sprouted legumes.
- Eat moderate amounts of citrus fruits and other low sweet fruits like papaya, guava, melon, pear, and apple.

Kidney Diseases
These can be classified into three types.

Acute Renal Failure
In this condition, the kidneys are unable to excrete the protein-breakdown by-products. Hence the diet has to be low in protein, of high biological value with adequate calories to prevent energy utilisation from tissue proteins. The fluid and electrolytes like sodium and potassium must be taken in measured amounts, according to the guidance of the dietician.

Chronic Renal Failure
This condition too requires diet to be tailored to individual needs. The intake has to be periodically adjusted depending on the biochemical test readings.

A person must follow these rules regarding diet:
- Take adequate quantities of energy foods.
- Replace, through diet the excessive quantities of water, sodium and potassium that have been excreted from the body.
- Monitor the ability of the kidneys to excrete the nitrogenous wastes, and salts.
- Take a low protein diet depending on that.
- A dose of multivitamin is helpful.

Nephrotic syndrome
The principal features of this condition are loss of albumin in urine, decrease in plasma albumin and marked edema (swelling).

A patient must:
- Compensate the urinary loss of albumin through a high protein diet.
- Counteract the edema through restricted sodium intake.

Obesity
Are you obese? Sneak a peek at the height-weight table as enumerated earlier. If you are gaining weight of 10% to 20% of the ideal body weight or more, then definitely you are obese and you are piling up problems at your doorstep. You are liable to develop diabetes, cardiovascular disorders, gall stones, varicose veins, abdominal hernia, flat foot, osteoarthritis of the spine, hips and knees.

Some precautions —
- Do not change your diet in a dramatic way. Conform to the basic food you are used to.
- Reduce the energy value of the diet.
- Eat sufficient quantity of protein, vitamins and minerals.
- Eat more of bulky, non-starchy foods.
- Stay away from sugar, honey, jam, sweets, chocolates, cakes, soft drinks, ice creams, fried foods, canned, and dried fruits and above all, alcohol.
- Help yourself to low calorie foods non-thickened soups, skimmed milk, roasted pappads etc.
- Exercise regularly since there is no substitute for it.

Anaemia

If you have anaemia, worry not you are not alone. Millions in India suffer from this complaint. Anaemia is caused when the normal synthesis of red blood corpuscles is disturbed, the common reasons being the deficiency of either iron, vitamin B12, folic acid or ascorbic acid.

Add on the following foods to overcome the deficiency:
- Iron can be derived from green and leafy vegetables, lentils, dates, figs, raisins, whole wheat, and jaggery.
- Folic acid is found largely in green leafy vegetables.
- Ascorbic also known as vitamin C is principally found in fresh fruits and vegetables. All citrus fruits are a rich source, but amla is said to be the best source of vitamin C.

(The above medical based information has been compiled from the bulletins of National Institute of Nutrition, ICMR, Hyderabad for gaining knowledge for a common man about importance of nutrients and curing diseases through balanced diet)

4
Time Management

Most of us are very poor in time management. The result is feeling of overloaded work, skipped schedule and accumulating tension. The truth is, if one can manage time effectively, he can accomplish twice as much the person who is poorly organised.

Considering the active average age of 65 years of a man, here is an interesting data calculated as how much time in the entire life one spends on working:

Activity	Years
Body rest and sleeping	23.5
Work activities	16.0
Personal direction	13.0
Travelling	4.5
Daily routine	4.5
Miscellaneous	3.5
Total	65.0

During the span of 16 years of work activities, if the time spent in unproductive work like gossiping, doing mistakes, redoing and waiting time etc., is eliminated, one would have hardly worked less than 10 years throughout the average life span of 65 years.

So, if you really need more than 365 days a year, 30 days in a month and 24 hours in a day, you can start using some quick time-management tips, which will help you to squeeze a few more precious minutes out of your day:

1. **Systematise morning hours:** Whether you are a businessman or a working person, the morning hours are very crucial to create stress that spoils the whole day. Arrange your morning hours in a systematic way and even minutes

are to be calculated in your routine activities, so that you get enough time to proceed for work place in time.

2. **Organise your personal belongings:** Don't waste time in trying to find your clothes/shoes etc., for example, open your wardrobe; quickly choose the clothes according to your taste/colour/fashion/season/day of the week. Don't waste your time on unwanted clothes, but weed them out and keep them aside to save the time.

3. **Daily personal belongings intact:** Keep all your personal belongings such as watch, car keys, office briefcase, shoes etc., at their proper place. The office files must be kept at their proper place and must not be left on the table to create confusion for the next day.

4. **Make realistic time schedule:** One must set a schedule, but the key word is realistic. Well-planned schedule will remind you to keep track of important hours, dates or events. You should prepare a list of activities, which are to be attended regularly.

5. **Be more assertive:** Learn how to be more assertive and manage your time properly. Most of us waste so much time in making excuses that we could not do this work due to shortage of time. Leave space in your schedule for the unexpected events.

6. **Plan all schedules only before lunch:** If you need to schedule meetings or appointments that have the potential to drag on indefinitely, try to schedule them right before lunch or near the end of the business day. With everyone thinking of getting away for lunch or for the evening, there's less potential for a marathon session.

7. **Buy non-perishable groceries and daily needed goods in bulk:** If space permits, buy non-perishable groceries and household goods in bulk which are to last at least for 2-3 months. Your visits to a general store will be reduced and you can save the time.

8. **Stock of petty things of frequent use:** You run out every time to purchase small items such as pen, refills and postage stamps etc. Buy them in enough quantity and save the precious time.

9. **Don't waste waiting time:** Don't waste your time on roadside or/at home to wait for anyone. This will be time

consuming and unnecessary tiring exercise. For the inevitable times when you must wait, find ways to put even a few minutes' waiting time to good use.

10. **Capitalise on your body rhythms:** When your body is mentally and physically at peak, try to use this time for the most demanding/important work. Due to your alertness when your body and mind is in the full form, you will be able to complete the assignment very quickly and will save your precious time.

11. **Priorities for medical appointments:** Make appointments for medical checkup well in advance and request for the earliest morning appointment which will save your whole afternoon time.

12. **Unwanted telephone calls:** If you're working at home or even trying to finish an immediate/necessary desk work in the office, keep the telephone on hold until the job is done. On the other hand avoid making/attending unwanted calls.

13. **Cultivate a friendly personality while at your desk:** Remain polite in the office, but unwelcome those who want to interrupt you when you're busy. Limit socialising to areas away from your workplace wherever possible.

14. **Unwanted web surfing:** We waste lot of time on unnecessary web surfing. We should be very specific to the subject to which web surfing is needed otherwise it takes number of hours to keep on finding the desired goal.

15. **Five minutes before sleep:** Spare only 5 minutes before sleep and remember the whole day's activities you have done or have left in between the work, which could not be finished due to some reason. Then take a glance at the priorities for the next day and plan accordingly.

5
Affirmations

Concept of Mind
Medical science has proved that only sickness and disease are the by-products of disturbed mind. Researches have also proven that stress, which breeds unnoticed in the mind, is one of the causes of all fatigue and illness, which will be noticed by the body probably at a very later stage. It is also now a well-established fact that we only use 10% of the total capacity of mind and don't even know how to use that properly. If we use its maximum potentiality, we would be perhaps in enhanced and healthier state and will live more productive lives.

Everyone is born with unique psychic abilities and powers and most of us are not even aware of them. Since our birth we have never learned how to master them and make their optimum usage but instead hoping for the best.

Our mind creates everything good and bad in life on the basis of perceptions of old habit pattern. The only reason we're not getting the most out of life is because we usually do not use or have the ability to use the power of our mind to create the things we exactly want. The mind is busy talking to itself keeping up an endless commentary about life, the world, our feelings, our problems, and thousand of other things. Most of the time we are not consciously aware of this stream of thoughts.

How Affirmations Influences the Mind
Throughout our life, we learn various activities or we are taught various activities like how to walk, how to talk, how to read, how to write etc., except the ability to use the mind power. If we really want to make change or improve our life, we must cultivate and work with our conscious mind, which has a direct link to your subconscious one. We must learn how to work with both so that they work together as a team, and then we will truly create the life we want. We have build huge walls around us, the need is thus to

understand ourselves and use our own inner strength. So most important is to develop our inner consciousness or intuition by tapping into the power of our subconscious mind by affirming positively and we'll generate amazing results in a very short time.

Affirmations are a useful method of "programming" the mind to act in a particular way. Human beings have the unique ability to define their identity, choose values and finally establish the beliefs. All this directly influences a person's behaviour. Conscious use of effective affirmations can modify the behaviour controlling factors resulting in different responses.

Affirmations can modify the working of your subconscious mind. Even when you feel things are hopeless, the spoken word can begin the healing. If you repeat a favourite affirmation, like a mantra, over and over and over again, crowding out all negative thoughts, and filling your mind with only one thought of conviction, you are doing something that is extremely effective in promoting change. The practice of doing affirmations allows us to replace some of our state of negative mind chatter with more positive ideas and concepts.

A fundamental principle of psychology is: "People are internally compelled to respond to situations in ways that will support or be consistent with their beliefs." A person's observations of his environment are filtered through his values to determine how to react to a person's beliefs, values and identity are usually acquired unconsciously based on his personal experience or observations of others' experiences to produce desirable or undesirable results in the environment.

The same process of repetition using affirmations can modify or create new beliefs about a person's identity. Longer the period of time, the affirmations are repeated, higher the priority they are given in a person's value system; and therefore the more they influence the person's behaviour to change.

A positive affirmation can lift your life and help achieving the goal. Such an affirmation sends the message to the universe, and the universe listens and responds in a positive manifestation of the desired wish. The affirmation must be a dedicated belief, not just an adhoc approach to "trying it out". One must be prepared to free himself from limiting insecurities and judgments and replace them with beliefs that have unlimited potential.

To understand how affirmations work, it's important to know and respect the "law of attraction." What you think about, you attract, even if it is negative. For instance, if you say, "I think I'm getting sick," then you will. If you think, "I don't want to get sick," then you probably will too. This is because you attract what you think. When you say, "I don't want to" or "I need," then you attract energies, which sustain the "need or don't want." In other words, you just never get there. Instead, say, "I feel great," or "my body is healthy in every way." You may have to fight your reasoning mind on this one, and repeat such an affirmation over and over until it clicks. But it truly works.

With affirming strongly you'll quiet your mind and develop your instincts or intuition while eliminating stress and enjoying greater fulfillment in every aspect of your life. You will accomplish goals you never dreamed possible. Your daily life becomes simple and easy. Stress, worry and anxiety disappear within days. You begin creating events you thought would never happen.

In order to give your affirmations a power or a chance to create the change you want, you have to eliminate the negative thoughts. Once you do this, you take charge of your life and begin creating massive changes quickly. So while you are using affirmations, try to temporarily suspend any doubts or disbelief you may have, at least for the moment and practise getting the feeling, which you desire, which is very real and possible.

Positive thinking is not just a philosophy, it is a practice you have to do every day over and over again. Affirmations are a great way to start developing positive thinking. Affirmations are sometimes necessary to override the negative opinions of ourselves that we have accumulated in our life's journey. In fact, positive affirmations need to be repeated more often in order to replace the old ones.

Once you say the affirmation, you must act as if it were true. For instance, regarding money, say a prosperity affirmation before writing, make sure you aren't vibrating a fear or anxious thought about money. And when you are in a store and see something you'd love, but don't think you can afford, never say "I can't afford it." Instead say, "I can have that."

Affirmations can be done silently, spoken aloud, written down or even sung or chanted. Even ten minutes a day of doing effective affirmations can counterbalance years of old mental habits. The more frequently you remember to be conscious of what you are "telling to yourself" the more positiveness you create for yourself.

Some Rules and Tips

Decide on a goal: Spend few minutes in a relaxing environment and think of your real desire. It may be career, self-love, improved health, gaining energy, a house, a relationship, a change in you, increased prosperity, a happier state of mind, beauty or better physical condition or whatever it may be.

First choose goals that are fairly easy for you to believe in, that you feel are possible to realise in the fairly near future. In this way you won't have to deal with too much negative resistance in yourself, and you can maximise your feelings of success as you practise regularly. Later when you have more practise, you can take on more difficult or challenging problems.

Create a clear idea or picture: Create an idea or mental picture of the object or situation exactly as you want it. You should think of it in the present tense as already existing, the way you want to be. Picture yourself with the situation, as you desire it now supported with details.

Focus on an idea and let your affirmation go: Trust your goal with love and focus on it until it is suppressed. Simply return to the affirmation gently once a day to boost your power. Generally in quite meditative or relaxed state of mind, more authentic and real ideas are generated. This is the time when it becomes an integrate part of your life and it becomes more of a reality to you.

Give a positive energy to the thought without fear: Believe that your desire is becoming true. Know that you truly deserve what you are asking for without guilt. Make strong positive statement to yourself, which exists, that it has come or is now coming to you.

Always use present tense: Always create your affirmation as it is becoming and visualise yourself in a situation as you want it. Affirming your desire in future tense will mean it is waiting to happen.

Use morning hours: While getting up in the morning or going to sleep at night when you are relaxed, are good times to use affirmations.

Positive words: As you focus on your goal, think about it in a positive, encouraging way. The universe does not acknowledge words such as 'not' or 'don't'. So, instead of saying "I am not weak" (the universe will only hear "I am weak"), say "I have enough energy and good health".

Be specific and short: Keep your affirmation focused on one key element at a time, without the clutter of many desires at once and be short and specific.

Repeat your affirmation: Write the affirmation by hand hundred and eight times, so that it has imprinted itself into your subconscious mind. Repetition means your desire can sink into every fiber of your being, settling naturally into your way of life.

Fix a time frame for each affirmation: Generally, practice every day minimum for 15 minutes to work with any single affirmation. For short goals it is recommended to practice for 21 days and for long-term goal minimum for 3 months or till its realisation. This is necessary for the message to sink to every corner of your self-perception. Dedicate your energy every time you repeat your affirmation.

It is generally either your early morning or late night hours to decide for affirmations. Sit comfortably and peacefully. Start observing your breathing for quite sometime and feel fully relaxed and detached from your body. This state of your subconscious mind is now ready to accept all suggestions and affirmations. Start chanting or repeating your affirmation as suggested above.

Some Common Affirmations

An affirmation can be any positive statement. There are thousands of possible affirmations; a few are enlisted to give you some idea so that you are able to form your own affirmations according to your need and desire:

- I am the master of my life and always in the right place at the right time, successfully engaged in the right activity.
- I am always relaxed, centred and peaceful; and have plenty of time for everything.
- I am naturally enlightened, an open channel of creative energy.
- I am dynamically self-expressive and communicate clearly and effectively.
- My memory is becoming photogenic, which grows better and better every day.
- I am honest with myself and find respectful ways to express my anger.
- I understand that everything is subject to change.

- I love and like to be loved and attracted towards loving, happy relationship; and my relationship with everyone is growing happier and more fulfilling every day.
- I now have enough time, energy, wisdom and money to accomplish all my desires.
- I am complete and getting better and better every day in every way. Courageous people are around me. I praise them patiently, gently and I am compassionate with them and myself.
- I am an enthusiastic speaker, well-prepared, logical, and sincere before any group.
- My mind is constantly creating optimistic and positive thoughts continuously.
- I am quickly and accurately decisive in all matters.
- Every day in every way I am getting better, better and better.
- The love inside me forgives everything.
- I am powerfully positive in everything I think, do and say.
- The universe is generous and gives me everything I need, every day.
- I am extremely rich in blessings, intelligence, character, wisdom, skills, and insight.
- I already possess within me anything I need to become and anything I want to be.
- I am very prosperous in all my business dealings.
- I am positive and prosperous in everything I do, every day.
- Because of my qualities, people are positively attracted to me. People seek me out to do business with them because they like my qualities.
- I possess an endless supply of creativity, energy and tolerance for any work or project that I assume.
- Prosperous people are attracted to me.
- I attract powerfully positive and healthy people into my life.
- I feel completely at ease and comfortable with all people.
- I am a winner in all my relationships.
- I have a rich collection of friends who value my qualities and I make valuable contributions to them also.
- I experience all my personal relationships with great consciousness.
- I am powerfully and intuitively guided with any changes in my personal relationships.
- I am wise, honest, thoughtful, healthy in my love relationships, and others treat me the same.

- I am extremely successful in my love relationships.
- I possess complete ability to express my feelings, intentions, thoughts in all my relationships and I express myself wisely.
- I am extremely successful in everything I do and say.
- I am the best judge of what is best for me, and I trust my judgement completely and I give myself the permission to do what I know is best.
- I am fully competent and capable in everything that I decide to do.
- I accept and acknowledge unconditionally my individuality and unique personality.
- I am highly creative, intelligent, attractive, energetic, witty, smart, healthy, wealthy, and wise.
- I am a self-determined person, and I allow others the same right.
- I do all my work with a free spirit and unlimited creativity.
- I always have a great source of energy for my work, because I am doing work that I love to do.
- I have just the right amount of time easily and comfortably to do all my jobs.
- I see all my work as opportunity to express myself, and develop to greater levels of achievement.
- Any work before me is a golden opportunity to learn, explore, develop, understand, contribute, achieve, build, promote, help, and become anything I desire.
- I am getting a peaceful sleep and awake fresh.
- My performance is getting better and better every day.
- I now eat all the right foods for optimum performance.
- I am confident and competent in my creative work.
- I have the courage and self-confidence necessary to put my solutions into practice.
- I am not fearful of anyone, though I give respect to everyone according to status.
- I recognise making mistakes but learn from my failures also.
- I treat each new problem as a new door to be opened and an opportunity to be creative.
- I forgive others and myself, release the past and move forward with love in my heart.

The above affirmations are time tested and have been used successfully to solve problems and enhance performance. It normally takes 40 days to change a habit; 90 days to confirm the change; after 120 days the change becomes a part of your life and after 1,000 days you are master of it.

6
Hypnosis

Much has been elaborated about stress in the earlier chapters. Now the main concern of this chapter is how hypnosis works to manage stress. Stress comes both from external and internal sources. It may come from the environment or from the body and by generating thoughts, but internally it is linked with sentiments or emotions, which are attracted or distracted only through the subtle vibrations. In reality our physical body is not composed of any matter at all; its basic component is a kind of force or essence, which we can call energy in the form of vibrations. So physically, everything within and around us looks solid but is made up of energy.

Normally, things appear to be solid and separate from one another on the level at which our physical senses perceive them. However, at atomic and subatomic levels, all solid matter is smaller and smaller particles within particles, which is just a pure energy. This energy is vibrating at different rates of speed and thus becomes different from finer to denser.

Manifestation is a Product of Thoughts

When we create something, we always create it first in a thought form. A thought or idea always precedes manifestation. "I intend an idea in my mind to write a book", which further precedes creation of all efforts at physical level. "I form a wish to have a new car", which gets manifesting at materialistic level and I buy a popular model", "I need a beautiful girl to marry" precedes finding out one by different means and so on.

An artist first has an idea or inspiration then only he draws a painting. An architect first plans and draws a design and then a house is constructed. The idea is like a blueprint, which creates an image of the form and further magnetises and guides the physical energy to flow into that form and eventually manifests it at the physical level.

Simply having an idea or thought, holding it in your mind, is an energy, which will tend to attract and create that particular form on the material plane. If you constantly think of illness, you eventually become ill even if you had no cause of it, if you believe yourself to be handsome, you are definitely so.

Thought is a relatively fine and light form of energy. It is quicker and faster even than sound and so it is easy to change. All forms of energy are interrelated and can affect one another. The energy of a certain quality or vibration tends to attract energy from a similar quality and vibration.

Stress is an accumulated form of negative energy, resulting in visible symptoms at gross level. Through hypnosis we can transform this negative energy into positive one for wholesome development of an individual. Thought being a quick, light and mobile form of energy manifests instantaneously, unlike the denser forms such as matter. Thought and feelings have their own magnetic energy, which can be moulded or transformed easily.

Reprogramming Subconscious Mind

When we are negative and fearful, insecure or anxious, we tend to attract the very experiences, situation or people that we are seeking to avoid. If we are basically positive in attitude, expecting and envisioning pleasure, satisfaction and happiness, we will attract and create situation and events, which conform to our expectations. So the more positive energy we put into imaging, the more it begins to manifest in our lives which is very much possible by reprogramming the subconscious mind.

The process of change does not occur on superficial levels, through mere 'positive thinking'. It involves exploring, discovering and changing our deepest, most basic attitude towards life. That is why learning to use creative visualisation in a hypnotic state can become a process of deep and meaningful growth.

At first you may practice creative visualisation at specific times and for specific goals. As you get more in the habit of using it and getting best results, you will find that it becomes an integral part of your thinking process. It becomes a continuous awareness, a state of consciousness in which you know that you are the constant creator of your life.

Concept of Hypnosis

Hypnosis is an altered state of consciousness, different from sleep or wakefulness. It is characterised by focused attention to a particular facet of mental activity with decreased global awareness.

A less technical definition of hypnosis is – "it is a naturally occurring altered state of consciousness in which the critical faculty is bypassed and acceptable selective thinking established. During this state of mind, affirmations/directions suiting to remove your deficiencies are put within the subconscious mind and after a continued practice, it works to improve the positivity the way you want." But there is no person or power on earth that can force you against your wish to be hypnotised, unless you yourself desire and follow the hypnotist's direction at your own will.

Hypnosis or rather self-hypnosis is useful to reduce the stress. To make it easier to understand how it works inside our brain, a little knowledge how our brain works, will be of best use. The left and right hemisphere of the human brain is engaged in different types of processing of data and input perceived through the senses. Left hemisphere is concerned with linguistic, logical and analytical, temporal and sequential thinking process. The modern educational systems and demands of socio-cultural environment have made us to use more and more of our left hemisphere.

The right hemisphere is concerned with imaginative or symbolic, creative and visual thinking process. The right brain has immense potential since it has total freedom in imagination, without any prior assumptions, while the left-brain being systematic, has limitations. So it is not absolutely necessary that an intuitive person can only be intellectual one, he may be operating from his right hemisphere mostly.

Our mind is like an iceberg, three fourth of which is subconscious, i.e., we are not consciously aware of the processes going on in this larger portion of our mind. The subconscious mind is the regulator of all our psychological processes and functions like behaviours and personality as well as biological processes and involuntary functions carried out by the internal organs. It possesses tremendous potentials, which are made available to an individual mainly through the functioning of right brain. Hypnosis provides systematic access to the right brain functioning and thereby awakening the deeper inner potentials.

The brain operates in four general states determined by the frequency of the electricity generated by the exchange of chemicals in the neural pathways. The four states include–full consciousness, hypnotic state, dream state and deep sleep state.

These four states correspond to electrical activity in the brain and are defined by frequency ranges on an EEG. Full consciousness occurs when the majority of the electrical activity in the brain is in the range of beta level 14-21 per second. The hypnotic state is a state when brain activity is in the frequency of alpha range of 8-13 per second. The dream State occurs when brain activity is in the theta range 4-7 per second and the deep sleep state occurs when brain activity is in the range of delta level 0.5-3 per second.

In the full awakening state, we are in beta range spending most of our time in full consciousness. In this state, our mind is fully attentive and uses logic to reason, evaluate, assess, judge and make decisions. At many crucial stages of our life, when making significant changes, the conscious mind often gets in the way.

In the hypnotic state, the gap between the conscious and the subconscious is minimised, so that memories stores in the subconscious mind are easily accessible, and new desired information is stored. In the hypnotic state, you are not really "thinking" in real sense, but rather in a very relaxed mood you are "experiencing" without questioning, without critical judgment or analysis. At this moment your conscious mind takes a back seat and subconscious mind operates. The hypnotist makes suggestions that are very likely to 'stick' precisely because your conscious mind is not getting in the way and you are not 'judging' or being 'critical' of the suggestions.

Self-hypnosis Induction

Dr B M Palan in his lectures has beautifully explained the self-hypnosis induction, sensory imagery conditioning, progressive muscular relaxations and ego strengthening. Merely reading books on hypnosis or just following the guidelines given hereunder do not make a person perfect to enter into the state of self-hypnosis. A personal training by an expert who would initially guide how to attain the state of hypnosis is absolutely necessary.

General Guidelines for Self-hypnosis Induction

Following are the general guidelines for self-hypnosis induction to use as and when needed in future after you have undergone a personal training. You have to add the desired suggestions after the induction.

- Make yourself comfortable on your seat or you may lie down.
- Close your eyes and relax your body.
- Be aware of the process of your breathing. Continue breathing normally, effortlessly. Feel, sense and experience the process of your breathing going on naturally.
- Decide in your mind "I will enter into a state of hypnotic trance by myself and will continue enjoying the same for 10 minutes. At the end of 10 minutes, I will come back to my normal awaking state of consciousness by counting slowly and silently from 5 to 1 in my mind."
- So let your breathing continue normally and automatically for a minute or so.
- Open your eyes slowly and stare at an imaginary spot on the wall in front of your eyes, a little higher than the eye level.
- Slowly, slowly let your eyes get closed.
- When your eyes get closed, let your whole body relax completely and then silently your mind goes into the alpha level.
- Imagine yourself in a pleasant and beautiful place where you may like to be.
- See and hear, feel and even smell all the beautiful things, which may be there. Fill your mind and heart with pleasure, joy and relaxation.
- When your mind reminds you about the time to come out, mentally come back from the imaginative pleasant place to the real place where you are conducting your self-hypnosis.
- Tell your mind, speak to yourself silently that– "Next time when I practice this self-hypnosis, I will go in a deeper state of trance, more easily and quickly."
- Count silently in your mind 5 to 1 while you may start feeling lightness in your eyes and alertness in your body. After finishing your count, as and when you feel like opening your eyes, you may open them slowly to be wide-awake, feeling refreshed in your body and mind.

Structured 8 Steps of Self-hypnosis

After learning induction, maintenance and termination of Self Hypnosis, you can start using the trance state for working towards your goals. Work on one goal at a time. Following are the 8 steps, which you can use as guidelines for an ideal structured self-hypnosis session. However, don't be very rigid about them. You can be flexible depending upon your style, purpose and time available to you for doing the session.

1. **Decide the 'work':** Finalise in your mind what you wish to do during the session. You will incline many suggestions and techniques. Select any one or two of them.
2. **Your own method of trance induction:** There is no single universal method of inducing self-hypnosis. After learning an induction technique from an expert, start practising in that way. By regular practice, you can introduce your own methods also.
3. **Use all senses together:** Try to involve all your senses (vision, hearing, touch, movements, smell and taste) while constructing a pleasant image. Make it as pleasant as you can.
4. **Actual work:** Do the work you decided in step 1 above and remember the suggestions/images float before your mental eyes.
5. **Continuation of pleasant imagery:** Once you complete the work, let the pleasant images be continued to enjoy good and pleasant feeling.
6. **Reorientation:** After a while reorient yourself to the place where you are doing self-hypnosis. Come back mentally from where you are, to the real present time and place accompanied all those good, positive feelings you imagined.
7. **Trigger words:** These are strong brief suggestions given during the trance towards authentic completion of work and after termination of trance, when you remember these trigger words, the same affirmation will continue to work in reality.
8. **Termination of trance:** Come out of the trance by giving a predecided signal silently in your mind by counting from 5 to 1. Take your own time and be slow in coming back to wide-awake state of your mind.

Preparing Your Own Hypnotic Suggestions

Few visualisation exercises based on symbolic images are briefed in this chapter. Each one of them opens the door to a new state of consciousness and can elicit specific psychological and biological changes. It is advisable to work few minutes daily for a week or so and then only shift to another. This will allow the dynamic imagery to gradually reveal for you the unnoticed inner realities and potentials.

Verbal (conscious) thinking also lightens your hypnotic trance. It is helpful to write down suggestions ahead of time so that you don't have to create them mentally while in trance. Before inducting trance, you can briefly review the suggestions that you wish to implant in your inner mind.

Sensory Imagery Conditioning

This is one of the most effective creative visualisation techniques used for working with situation-based problem. When you want to alter undesirable specific situation and make desirable changes in your usual, set pattern of thinking, feeling or behaviour, only then you can use this technique.

Conditioning means forming a habit. Here, you are going to form a new, desirable habit of thinking, feeling and/or behaving through creating specific sensation and rich images in your inner mind.

Following are the 4 steps of this technique. Learn them and while using the technique, you may use your own creatively to produce relevant images. Feel free to be flexible.

Step: 1 Follow all guidelines for going into a state of deep trance as explained under self-hypnosis induction.

Step: 2 Under the self-hypnotic state, imagine yourself in your inner mental tranquility room, sitting comfortably on a sofa. Watch a movie on the TV screen there. It is the video recording programmed on you while you were undergoing your problem situation. Find yourself on the TV screen. You were undergoing your usual, stereotyped negative experience in this movie. Watch yourself behaving in unhealthy and undesirable manner. Be aware of thinking and feelings perceived by you on the TV screen. You are facing the problem...you are suffering there. But, see gradually, this movie is fading away...becoming black and while, small and far off. The sound track is also not clear. Continue this for a couple of minutes (use this step only once or twice for any problem and then you may do only step 3 and 4 for achieving the desired goal).

Step: 3 Put off the TV Go near the video player and take off the cassette, which is an older one. Insert a newly programmed cassette in its place. Come back and sit comfortably. Now you are going to watch your new movie seeing yourself undergoing the same experience once again. But now it is with healthy and desirable behaviours. Sense the positive, more appropriate thinking and feelings generated in you on the screen. Bring some close-ups. Make the picture bright and colourful with a very clear sound track. Continue watching your positive movie for about 5 minutes.

Step: 4 While step 3 is in progress, keep in your mind the following two post-hypnotic suggestions:
  a) "Day by day I am able to experience these healthy images of myself more and more clearly...vividly...during my self-hypnosis session."
  b) "I am gradually merging with this image. I am creating the internal reality, which is becoming an external reality, gradually and naturally. So, even in my normal waking state of consciousness, day by day, I am getting appropriate positive thoughts and more comfortable feelings under such circumstances. This is making my behaviour...my actions...more and more desirable as each day is passing."

Dynamic Imageries

There are thousands of imagery creations based on symbolic images and you can also make your own too. Each one of them opens the door to a new state of consciousness and can elicit specific psychological and biological changes in the body.

It is advisable to stay with one creation for few minutes daily for a week or so first following the steps in the sensory imagery conditioning technique and then only shift to another. One can also form one's own imagery creative visualisation, so here are few suggestions given for your guidance:

Dynamic personality, positive attitude and strengthening concentration

"I am forceful, vibrant, and energetic and have the power to attain my goals...Day by day I am becoming more and more aware of my inner strength"

"I have great inner courage and project a positive self-image...I am optimistic and enthusiastic...I am always ready to accept new challenges and emerge as a winner."

"Total concentration is mine...I have the power and ability to focus my concentration at will...I remain alert and focused...I easily block all thoughts related to what I am working on...My goal of super concentration is easily achieved" (use *'inner strength, concentration'* as trigger word).

Enhance psychic ability, quick thinking and brainpower

"Day by day my psychic abilities are opening up...up...and...up... I am able to develop my extra sensory perceptions and sixth sense... I am becoming more telepathic and clairvoyant."

"I get what I want with quick thinking and respond with best answers..I am mentally alert and attentive..I think and react quickly to problems and use the power of my mind to the fullest."

"Day by day my brain is becoming suppler and alert...suppler and alert...My learning abilities and performance are increasing...I think more clearly and more creatively."

Enhance creativity, self-discipline, self-confidence and self-esteem

I am becoming more and more creative and innovative...I drew creative inspiration from the universe and release unlimited power of my creative ability.

"I have the self-discipline to accomplish my personal and professional goals...I direct my time and energy to manifest my desires and increase my self-discipline taking control of my life."

"I am self-reliant, self-confident, full of independence and determination...I have great courage and project a very positive self-image...Every day I am becoming more self-confident."

"I am a self-directed, self-confident winner...I believe in my abilities and enjoy high self-esteem, positive self-image, generate success and happiness...I am proud of myself and do things that make me proud positively."

Elimination of stress and empower inner peace

"I am surrounded with peace and relaxation...I am at peace with myself, the world and everyone in it..I am physically and emotionally relaxed and in complete balance and harmony...Ultimate relaxation is mine."

"I am at peace with myself, the world and every one around me...I accept unchangeable things the way they are...My mind is calm and has all I need...I now feel calm, balance and harmonious... I experience tranquility, love and joy (use 'Peace, balance and harmony' as trigger words)."

Pain removal, insomnia, weight loss and healthy lifestyle
"Day by day in every way I am becoming healthier and healthier.... My immune system has become stronger and functions at optimum efficiency and keeps me healthy...I choose perfect health and release full power of my mind."

"Day by day I am getting relaxed and feel good. I am mentally healing myself, with every exhaling the pain is released."

"Peaceful sleep has become reality for me now. I fall asleep easily and sleep well. I am sleeping peacefully throughout the night... I wake up relaxed and refreshed."

"I am slim, trim and maintain healthy body and lead a healthy lifestyle...I eat only healthy and nutritious food in smaller portions and stick to my diet. ('Relaxed and release, peaceful sleep' are the trigger words)."

Removal of addiction (especially alcohol)
"I have the will power and discipline to do anything I desire...I can mould my desire according to my wish...I ignore all cravings and insecurity...I am letting go of the past and freeing myself, enjoy deep inner peace and love for myself."

"I have stopped drinking to feel better mentally and physically... I do not get attracted towards alcohol (you can add desired addiction to be removed)...I have the inner strength to turn away from alcohol... I have stopped drinking to improve my relationship and thinking."

Guilt release, worry and fear, relationship improvement, forgive and forget and emotional detachment
"I am at peace and have forgiven myself...I learn from the past to create a positive future...Every day I am at peace... I am feeling better and better."

"I am far away from worry and fear...I do not let those thoughts affect me...I am confident and secure...I am calm and optimistic... I feel powerful and in full control of myself...I am peaceful, balanced and harmonious...My mind is calm and thinks positively."

"My relationship with people is getting better and better...Day by day it is becoming harmonious and friendlier...I directly and honestly communicate and share my views with others...I communicate, accept others as they are without expectations...I experience good relationship, excitement and joy with people around me."

"I forgive and release my anger and expectations...I allow negativity to flow through me without affecting...every day I find it easier to forgive and release my expectations from others...I am liberating myself..." (use 'Peaceful Mind, Forgive and Release' as trigger words).

"I mentally detach myself from all people I do not like..I detach from everything that does not work for me...I drew joyous new experiences in my life...I am optimistic and confident about my future." (use "Detach" as trigger word).

Wealth and success, goal accomplishment, satisfaction and happiness

"I explore best possible ways to become wealthy. I have a desire to be wealthy and successful...I am persistent, ambitious and determined..I do not become miser but I plan my expenditure and respect money."

"I have the power to do more things in less time..I am increasing my speed and productivity..My time is valuable and I use it efficiently to accomplish my goals fully."

"I create my own space for satisfaction and happiness in my life...I am happy and satisfied with what I have and what I get...I accept what I cannot change and change what I can...I have the power and ability to create any reality I desire to live...I am happy and satisfied." (use 'Happy and satisfied' as key words).

Progressive Muscular Relaxation

The purpose of this exercise is to rise above the limited identification with body, mind and intellect to bring about wholesome development of one's own self. It is also called Shav Asana.

- Make yourself comfortable, you may sit on a comfortable chair or you may lie down. Keep your eyes quietly closed. You can adjust yourself to be in a comfortable pose.
- While your body is resting comfortably with your eyes quietly closed, you just attend to the process of your breathing. Your normal and natural breathing which is going on all by itself. Just feel and sense the process of your breathing and see every time as you are breathing out your body is relaxing more and more.

- And while your breathing may continue normally naturally going all by itself, just be aware of your right leg. If necessary you may move it around and lose you right leg.
- Be aware of the relaxation in your right foot and right ankles and see how beautifully your right leg muscles and the knee joints are relaxing and all the way upto the hip joint whole of your right leg is relaxing more and more.
- And now you may be aware of the relaxation in your left leg. You may move around if necessary and leave the whole weight of your left leg to be supported on to the support.
- And be aware of the relaxation in the left foot, left ankles joint, leg muscles and the knee joint and all the way upto the hip joint. Whole of your left leg is relaxing more and more.
- And now both of your legs would continue to relax more and more. In the meantime imagine, think in your mind about the waves of relaxation and comfort–waves of relaxation and comfort have started from your legs spreading up on your stomach and lower back, chest and upper back waves after waves of relaxation and comfort are encircling your stomach and the lower back, chest and the upper back...and all the muscles of your trunk are also relaxing more and more.
- And as your trunk muscles continue to relax more and more you be aware of the relaxation in your right arm. See how beautifully your right arm is resting on to the support limply and loosely.
- Be aware of relaxation in your right shoulder, elbow, wrist, hand and fingers.
- And as your right arm continues to relax even more– now you be aware of the relaxation in your left arm. Feel relaxation at the left shoulder, elbow, wrist, hand, and fingers.
- You are just keeping the weight of your arms to rest limply and loosely on to the support.
- And while your arms continue to relax more and more, see how your neck is relaxing, as your neck muscle is relaxing more and more. If your head is drooping, you may allow it to droop and allow it to fall, if it is falling, allow your head to rest now comfortably.
- The neck muscles would continue to relax more and more. Now be aware of the relaxation of the face and see how

your forehead is becoming smooth and soft, loose, limply relaxed.
- Early in the morning if you look at the steel and silent surface of the water in the pond, you may find as if the water is sleeping in the pond.
- Absolutely waveless, something like that you are sensing in your forehead steel and silence, soft and loose and relaxed forehead.
- Be aware of relaxation in both your eyelids and be aware of the relaxation in your upper limb and lower limb.
- And as you are aware of the relaxation on your lips and if your mouth wants to open a little bit, allow it to open–your chin is relaxing, the lower jaw is also relaxing.
- Be aware of the relaxation in your right cheek and left cheek–every part of your face is relaxing more and more.
- And the whole body right from the tips of your toes to the top of your head is relaxing more and more, every muscle, every joint of your body is getting into a deeper and deeper state of relaxation and comfort.
- As your body is relaxing more and more, see how your mind is relaxing, calm and serene, serene and calm, more peaceful, tranquil.
- Your breathing is becoming slow and regular, regular and slow. You may now like to once again be aware of the process of your breathing.
- And as you are sensing your breathing–if there is other thought peeping in your mind let it come. You don't want to prevent the thought. Do not fight with the thought. The thought may come and the thought may go.
- You know when the bird flies through the sky, it leaves no footsteps behind. The bird may come, the bird may go, leaving no footsteps behind, leaving the sky as it is calm and serene.
- The thought may come and the thought may go leaving no footsteps behind because your mind is learning to be like the sky remaining calm and serene, serene and calm.
- So whenever it is easily possible just keep on sensing the process of your breathing. Gradually the breathing is getting slow and regular.
- Day by day as you continue practising progressive muscular relaxation you will find that your body is learning to go in

a deeper state of relaxation easily and naturally. Whenever you practice your mind is learning to drift in a peaceful and tranquil, more calm and serene, enjoyable state.
- And now you may feel lightness in your eyes, comfortable sensation of lightness in your head and a pleasant feeling of alertness and archives feeling through your body. When you feel waves of alertness and archives flowing through your body and you feel a comfortable lightness in your eyes. Taking your own time you may slowly open your eyes to find freshness in your body, and mind. Take your own time and be slow.

Mini nap

Beata Jencks described this technique of giving good rest to the body and mind in a brief period of time. It is a very useful technique and it can be effectively utilised whenever you are tired and feeling sleepy but you do not want to sleep due to any reason.
- Put aside your work and sit comfortably on a chair and close your eyes.
- Attend to the process of your breathing. Just feel the process of your normal and natural breathing for about a minute or so.
- Then start associating some thoughts, as under, with every breath which you are letting out:
  1. First breath out–"One minute is passing and I am sleeping"
  2. Second– "I am sleeping for the last two minutes."
  3. Third– "I am enjoying a beautiful sleep for the last four minutes."
  4. Fourth– "It is a nice, deep and sound sleep which I am enjoying for the last eight minutes."
  5. Fifth– "Quarter of an hour has passed. I am enjoying good sleep."
  6. Sixth– "I am sleeping for the last half an hour. It is good deep sleep."
  7. Seventh– "I am enjoying a very deep and sound sleep for the last one hour."
  8. Eighth– "I enjoyed a wonderful sleep for the last two hours."
- After reaching upto two hours in your mind, say silently to yourself– "After these two hours I am sensing the waves of

alertness and energy throughout my body. I am feeling like waking up now."
- Then slowly open your eyes. Take one or two deep refreshing breaths. Stretch your body and be absolutely wide-awake to start your work.

Ego Strengthening

Concept of 'Self'

Every individual is recognised as a 'Self' which has a body and a mind, whereas an 'I' is a pure consciousness. In fact the 'Self' itself is neither the body nor the mind. The body and mind are merely the extensions through which the 'Self' exists and interacts in the world by which the consciousness is depicted. The whole physical world is nothing but depiction of the same consciousness.

Assumptions/beliefs of mind

The body performs two tasks for the 'self'. One, it detects and transmits information through its sense organs about the external and internal environment to the mind. The second function is to execute the actions. On the basis of information recorded, the mind performs the tasks of generating the cognition and effect for the 'Self' during its existence and interactions in the world. As time passes, on the basis of these cognition and affects, the mind forms certain assumptions, beliefs and attitudes, which remain stored in the mind. In specific situations, through the cognition and effect, the mind makes certain decisions in the light of the relevant assumptions, beliefs and attitudes for execution of specific actions.

Formation of Ego

Among several assumptions and beliefs developed by the mind, most of them attribute polishing the so called 'Self' in an 'Image' form. The beliefs, attitudes and assumptions pertaining to the 'Image' strongly constitute the ego. The ego in other words is the sum total of assumptions/beliefs and attitudes developed by the mind regarding the elution of 'Image'. Being an egoistic personality is not always bad, but the consideration is, what assumptions/beliefs are forming the so-called ego. It is classified in two terms viz., *high ego* and *low ego*.

High ego strength (Pure ahankar)

When the mind holds positive and healthy beliefs about the 'self' that 'I' is a pure and perfect, eternal blissful consciousness and whatever limitations/problems are there, they belong either to the body or to the mind. The mind of this person remains full of joy and serenity, peace and security. The external, worldly matters may cause fewer disturbances. 'Me' is very small thing for this individual's mind and that too just for a short period on the surface only, while deep within the mind there is continuous flow of joy and serenity.

Such an individual remains calm and comfortable for most of the time, irrespective of the circumstances. An uninterrupted and continuous flow of blissful consciousness flows into his mind as well as body. In the background buffering of this blissful consciousness, the mind and body function in harmony with each other, ultimately to the advantages of the pure 'self' and surrounding environments, which is classified as '*Pure Ahankar*'.

A person having high ego strength has the following characteristics:

- He is positive in thinking and objective in his apprehension of the external world and in self-knowledge.
- His activity is organised over a longer time-span and, thus is able to maintain schedules and plans.
- He can resolve and choose decisively among alternatives.
- He is not overwhelmed by his drives but can direct them into socially useful channels.
- He can resist immediate environmental pressures while contemplating and choosing a self-selected course.

Low ego strength (Impure ahankar)

Under certain circumstances, an individual may have weak or negative beliefs about the 'self'. Many a times, the mind imposes/inflicts its own limitations on the 'self' (e.g. "I am weak", "I can't do this or that") which makes a person at low ego. Many individuals having vast knowledge and intellect set their stage at a very high level and cannot land at all. They think themselves always at the height of their 'self image' with no comparison with others, resultantly they always humiliate others. This imposition is due to the ignorance in the mind regarding the real form of the 'self'.

It may be imagined that in this situation the flow of blissful consciousness is obstructed into the mind and body and loses harmony with the 'Self'. The mind would then function on its own, thinking and feeling whatever it prefers and feel without considering the interest or advantage of the individual 'self'. Also the mind may function in a self defeating way, making body functions against the interest of the 'self'. The external worldly affairs would cause severe turmoil in the mind due to lack of existence of blissful consciousness. This individual under such circumstances is said to have *'Impure Ahankar'*.

A person is indicative of the following by his behaviour for low ego:
- The ego weak individual is more like a child whose behaviour is impulsive and immediate.
- His perception of reality and 'self' is distorted.
- He is less capable of productive work because his energy is drained out for protection of wrapped and unrealistic self-concepts.
- Negative thinking and conflict may burden him.
- Becomes most self-centred person.
- Behaves abnormally with people in the society.

Ego-strengthening exercise
To eliminate the negative effects on low ego possessed persons it is necessary to re-enunciate the general ego-strengthening suggestions, which we call ahankar purification suggestions by exercising the following:
- Make yourself comfortable on a chair or you may lie down. Keep your eyes quietly closed. You may move around if necessary to make you even more comfortable.
- And now observe the process of your breathing, your normal and natural breathing, which is going on all by itself. You just feel and sense the process of your breathing and see how beautifully your body is relaxing more and more. With every breath you are letting out.
- While your body may continue relaxing more and more you may now like to open your eyes slowly. Look straight a little up on the wall or on the ceiling in front of your eyes. As you keep on staring over there at some imaginary point, whenever you are ready to go in a state of trance, let your eyes get closed. Whenever you think, you feel that ok now I am ready, let your eyes get closed. Let your eyes get closed perfectly.
- And now you relax your eyelids. Let them be more loose so that they would like to stay closed and do not wish to

open. And when your eyes are relaxed to the point that they like to stay closed, you relax them even more. Let them be further relaxed. Let them be more loose limb so that you are sure that they cannot open.
- While your eyes are relaxing, you allow your body to go in a deeper and sound state of relaxation and comfort, let the whole body, the entire body right from the tips of your toes, all the way to the top of your head. Get into a deeper and sounder state of relaxation and comfort.
- Let every muscle, every joint of your body relaxed more and more.
- And while your body may continue relaxing more, your mind continues with positive images created in the mind all by itself effortlessly while the body continues relaxing more and more.
- And in this calm and quite, relaxed and comfortable state of mind, you may like to imagine yourself being in a beautiful garden. Just picture yourself being in a beautiful garden.
- Imagine there is greenery all around, beautifully maintained number of flowers of different kinds and colours.
- Beautiful multicoloured butterflies flying here and there tall trees, and birds singing under and over those trees.
- The atmosphere is very pleasant and delightful, cool and comfortable breeze of air coming from over the rose plants , bringing sweet fragrances of roses for you and you are just roaming about leisurely in this beautiful garden.
- There is something very interesting happening now, there is a rainbow in the sky. The rainbow starting from the horizon far away reaching up in the sky. This end of the rainbow is coming down, down right up to your feet, right in front of you.
- You can see those beautiful colours of the rainbow from very near–violet, indigo, blue, green, yellow, orange, and red.
- And as you are watching the rainbow see how effortlessly you have started climbing up on the rainbow. Effortlessly you are just climbing up and up on the beautiful seven coloured divine path of the rainbow.
- Up you go, more safe and secure, peaceful and tranquil. You feel climbing up and up very safely, reaching up on the top of the rainbow.

- There is a beautiful divine atmosphere. There is a white bright light all around you and as you are breathing in this light is entering in your body, the white light filling your lungs and your heart making them healthier.
- And the light is spreading up through your neck, penetrating through your brain, reaching in every corner of your head, to every neuron, every new cell of your brain. While they are coming in contact with this bright light, cool and comfortable light, they are becoming more healthy functioning in perfect health and beautiful harmony.
- The light is further spreading down in your abdominal cavity, filling your stomach and intestines, penetrating through your lever, and kidney, pancreas and every organ within your stomach making them more and more healthy.
- And the bright and white, cool and comfortable light is spreading down and down through your shoulders into your arms penetrating all the way upto the tips of your toes, upto the tips of the fingers making every tissue of your body, every cell of your body to function in a healthy manner and in beautiful harmony.
- This bright white, cool and comfortable light all around you and within your body seems as if it is an ocean, ocean in you and me and every one of us. The whole ocean is merging.
- And in this very pleasant and positive state of your mind, deep within the depth of your mind, these thoughts are floating. That day by day my mind is learning to be more calm, quiet, serene, and comfortable, irrespective of the happenings and situations.
- And my mind is learning to remain calm, quiet, serene and comfortable. The worldly affairs, external happenings may sometime create some little temporary waves, externally. But deep within the depth of my mind there is always peace and tranquility.
- Day by day I am becoming more calm and more relaxed, peaceful and comfortable. These thoughts may rebarbate in the depth of my mind, while you are enjoying on the top of the rainbow, in the divine atmosphere.
- And then there may be thoughts floating in your mind, that day by day my mind is realising my own potentials,

- capabilities and my mind is developing faith in me and becoming a self-confident individual as each day passes.
- And now you may slowly start sliding and gliding down in that seven coloured beautiful path of the rainbow and the rainbow is landing you back, very slowly and safely in the beautiful garden.
- You may now find the garden more alive, the leaves of the trees are more green, the colour of the butterflies are more sparkling, the fragrance of the flowers are more sweeter and the touch of the breeze and air is more fresh.
- Collect all the wonderful feelings–the feeling of joy and cheerfulness, the feeling of peace and tranquility. Collect all these beautiful feelings in your mind and in your heart.
- And then you may slowly fly, float and drift mentally back over here where your body is resting and relaxing comfortably with your eyes quietly closed.
- Whatever positive and healthy thoughts, emotions, and images were created in your mind during this session, have a great influence, tremendous impact upon your thoughts, feelings, and behaviour.
- These thoughts will have greater influence upon your body and mind consistently even when you are in the awaking state of consciousness. Wherever you are and whatever you are doing or the next time whenever you do your self-hypnosis, you will be drifted in a deeper state of trance, more enjoyable state of body and mind, easily and naturally.
- Now slowly your eyes will start feeling lighter. There is a comfortable sensation of lightness in your head and pleasant feeling of alertness and archives flowing throughout your body. Whenever you feel the same alertness and archives spreading throughout your body, whenever you feel comfortable lightness in your eyes, take your time, you may slowly, slowly, open your eyes, feeling good and refreshing in your body and in your mind. Take your own time and be slow.

7
Meditation

Meditation has been used over the years in many parts of the world to achieve deep relaxation and piece of mind. It is not a religion or philosophy but a tool that utilises our internal awareness to release tensions, gain self-confidence and peace. Basically each human being seeks happiness and prosperity in the materialistic world to fulfill his desire of high status, power, good relationships etc. Failing to what he seeks for; he reverts back to the internal realm through meditation in order to understand the real happiness, which already exists. His search for fulfillment of aspiration inclined him towards meditation, which is often accompanied by numerous crises and difficulties for beginners when he practises.

Though the main aim of the simpler meditation is to gain the mental peace, but practising higher level of meditation not only increases the efficiency but also increases our interest toward routine activities. The difference between the simpler and higher form can be easily noticed in each and every phase of our life.

Misconceptions about Meditation
Generally meditation is considered to be a difficult task to be performed easily and successfully by everyone. Most of the people are of the view that entering into meditation; one has to get rid of all the worldly things like profession and family etc. Hence, it is quite clear that people are not yet fully aware of meditation and still have lot of misconceptions about it.

Our mind is mingled with evil thoughts, so we are unable to see things in their proper nature. We do not see reality, but we see things as we would like them to be. For example, we perceive our bodies as objects of beauty, so we spend much of the time and effort to decorate it with fine clothes, cosmetics and perfume etc. This does not mean that we have to give up conventional activities. We still have to live in society and carry out certain actions like caring for our bodies and maintaining personality. Meditation enables us to see things as they are, devoid of our preconceived ideas, projections, likings, and dislikings. We are no longer attached to them and see them as medium of functioning in the world. It leads eventually to the attainment of the highest wisdom.

Some people think that meditation is only for those who have problems, which needs to be sorted out. This is, however, a serious misconception as it ignores the very positive contribution of meditation for a common man. The practice of meditation helps to prevent us from becoming upset when difficulties arise and it develops beneficial qualities such as courage, energy and vision. It helps us to cultivate the happy responses and reduce the unhappy ones. In addition to the mental benefits, the practice of meditation also improves physical health.

There are descriptions in our ancient books about saints who used to meditate for years together in order to seek spiritual bliss and resultantly their physical condition would deteriorate which counted as a major reason for the misconception about meditation. However, in reality the main aim of meditation is just to achieve mental awareness by looking deeper inside oneself.

Meditation is something that must be experienced. No matter how many books you have read, but it is only a practice, which counts. It is a technique through which one gets an insight into his inner sense, his potentials and observes himself from every angle and perspective. It is a way to examine the reality of one's body and mind, to identify unsolved hidden problems and to develop unused potential, to channelise for liberalisation.

It aims at cleansing the impurities and disturbances of mind, such as lustful desires, hatred, anger, jealousy, pride, arrogance, ill-will, worries, restlessness and transforming them into pure and natural qualities such as love, compassion, kindness, concentration, awareness, determination, energy, confidence, joy, and tranquility.

Role of Meditation in Stress Management

Through continuous practice, meditation guides us not only to relax the body and mind, but also to focus away from stressful thoughts and feelings, and that is considered to be a very effective tool in stress management. You will find that a relaxed state of concentrated mind will do wonders even under any adverse circumstances. Remember that you lead the main role to generate stress for yourself and later suffer from it. Change your cognitive processing and develop mindfulness and concentration through meditation, and learn to focus on the present.

Meditation, yoga or other spiritual practices help us to discover the sufferings and the manner through which one liberates from it. All these teach us to observe the inner functioning from a neutral point of view. Meditation is a state achieved from intense concentration on a single object until all other thoughts vanish and an intense awareness, peace and calmness is left. Through meditation, the right understanding is built, that all objects, indeed everything in the world is ever changing and is impermanent. The suffering associated with grief, for example, is caused by an emotional attachment to individuals without accepting the fact of the impermanent nature of life. Thus the most important thing is to learn how to reduce stress through meditation. It teaches us to stay in present and enables to pay full attention to enjoy the life even better than before, as your life at that moment deserves your undivided attention.

In Patanjali's, *Yoga Sutras* the meditation is described as one of the eight limbs of yoga. *Dhyana* (meditation) is considered the highest practice and final step before bliss. Meditation means sensible withdrawal (*pratyahara*) and concentration (*dharana*), determined contemplation (*dhyana*), with the aim of triggering a superconscious state (*samadhi*), which is one of the intuitive awareness of the identity of cosmic soul. Accordingly samadhi may be a long time process, but it helps to reduce stress and anxiety, lowers blood pressure and improves concentration, clarity and creativity and apart from this, it has lot of other benefits also.

Significant Biological and Psychic Factors

Meditation is a state of relaxed state of body and peaceful mind together. So before experiencing this sacred way to release stress and achieve ultimate happiness, one must understand the human biology and influence of mind on it. Some important facts and medical findings by renowned doctors and researchers are put forth which one should know.

Biochemistry of the body is a product of awareness

The hypothalamus gland in human brain produces different types of chemicals, which after mixing in the blood ultimately react on the body. Beliefs, thoughts and emotions first influence the functioning of this gland which then create the chemical reactions that uphold and change life in every cell. The biochemistry of the body is a product of awareness expressed by beliefs and thoughts. Thus this mechanism of mind while influencing every cell in the body alters the structure every moment. Our body then responds the way our mind dictates, like growing of cells in the body can speed up, slow down or even the process of growing old can reverse.

We human beings are the only creatures on earth that can transform the biology, the way we feel and think. Our nervous system is constantly aware of the happenings in the body and interferes the body cells through thoughts. Even a short period of depression can cause disorder in the immune system and on the other hand falling in love can improve it. Despair and hopelessness through thoughts raise the risk of heart attack and cancer, thereby shortening life, on the other hand joy and fulfillment keep us healthy and make life longer.

If we correlate biology and psychology, it seems to be a perception which appears to be automatic, but in fact it is a learned trend. The world you live in, including the experience of your body, is completely dictated by how you learned to perceive it. By changing your perception, you can change the experience of your body and your world you live around.

Urge of intelligence creates your body into a new form every second. Although each person seems separate and identical but all of us are connected to patterns of intelligence that govern the whole universe. So you are much more than the boundaries of your body, ego and personality. The rules of cause and effect as you accept them have compressed you into the size of a body, but in reality you are not limited to it.

Transformation of new body
The universal energy transforms itself every moment. Our body follows the same creative impulse resulting in more than 6 trillion reactions taking place in each cell every moment. Our body would fall into disorder and weaken if flow of this change stops. To keep body healthy and alive change of formation is necessary.

By appearance your body appears to be composed of solid matter that can be broken down into molecules, but quantum physics tells us that our body is a collection of atoms only and every atom has more than 99 per cent empty space. The atomic and subatomic articles are moving at lightening speed through this space, which is actually a bundle of vibrating energy only.

Every moment you are exhaling atoms of hydrogen, oxygen, carbon and nitrogen that were forming a solid matter inside the body as part of your kidney, stomach, liver, pancreas, heart, lungs and brain. These are vanishing into thin air and being replaced as quickly and endlessly as they are being broken down. Due to this change, the skin replaces itself once a month, the stomach lining every five days, the liver every six weeks and skeleton every three months. In a span of one year, 98% of the atoms in your body get exchanged for new ones. These organs appear same from moment to moment, but they are always in flux.

There is unbelievable liberation of change in your body. Simply by changing your perception, you can make drastic and incredible changes in your body. How you perceive yourself causes immense changes in the body. For example, a mandatory retirement at 58, sets a random cut off date for active physical contribution for social usefulness. Till the day before attaining the age of 58, the person contributes labour and value to the society, and thereafter he becomes dependent.

This perception medically results in many diseases. Statistics have shown that the rate of heartattack and cancer is higher among those who have just retired. But by accepting the life as a part of social fabric, if elders change their perception, they may remain extremely vigorous like they can do lifting, climbing and stay more energetic that we sometimes do not accept as normal.

Conscious control over in voluntary functions

The automatic mechanism inside the body's so-called involuntary nervous system is designed to control functions that have slipped out of your awareness. If you begin walking beside the road carelessly, the involuntary centres in your body would still be coping with the world, keeping on the look out for danger, poised to activate the stress response at a moment's notice.

Hundred of functions continue ceaselessly without your voluntary control for which you even pay no attention like respiration, digestion, growing and repairing cells, purifying toxins, preserving hormonal balance, converting stored energy from fat to blood sugar, maintaining stable blood pressure and body temperature, balancing as you walk and sensing movements and sounds in the surrounding environments etc.

Living unconsciously leads to numerous deteriorations, while alert and conscious participation prevents this unnecessary destruction. Paying conscious attention to bodily functions instead of leaving them on automatic running will transform how you improve at body level. Every so-called involuntary function from heartbeat and breathing to digestion and hormone regulation is only possible through consciousness by meditation.

Metabolism

Metabolism is an intelligent act more than a burning of sugar. The human body derives its primary energy by burning sugar, which is transported to the cells in the form of glucose or blood sugar. The chemical structure of glucose is closely related to common sugar tablet sucrose, but you don't get the energy if you burn this sugar tablet. In every physical action the energy is required which is attained through burning of cells and get more through blood sugar for formation of new cells.

Thus the process of metabolism is simply the burning of old cells during body functions and formation of new cells. It is observed that during meditation the metabolism rate gets slowed down and supply of oxygen for burning is required at a very low level which keeps the heart beat rate decreasing on an average of three beats a minute and that the rate of breathing gets slow, deep, rhythmic, effortless, and smooth. Slow breathing is always helpful to reduce stress and gives longer life as is obvious from the table below:

Creatures	Breathing rate/ Per Minute	Average life span in years
Dog	45-50	12
Cow	25	28
Man	8-16	80
Tortoise	2	170

So if you want to change your body, change your awareness first, change the way of your thinking. You fall victim of sickness, ageing and early death because you lose awareness, intelligence and control over the end product of intelligence i.e., the human body.

Mind is a big healer

Whenever thought goes, it carries a chemical with it, for example a depressed person is more likely to get sick, because his mental state creates certain biochemicals which are harmful and generate diseases. It is understood that the body is capable of producing any biochemical response. The mind once gives the appropriate suggestion, it works on the body since both mind and body are interdependent on each other.

One of the functions for example, has already been explained above on the working of hypothalamus gland in the brain. It is a central control room of the body structure, which coordinates the body's nervous system affecting metabolism in the body. In summer days for example, if blood heats up as little as a tenth of a degree, the hypothalamus gland sends messages to the pituitary gland through the sympathetic nervous system to dilute surface blood vessels to open thousands of sweat glands situated just under the skin layer.

On the other hand if blood temperature drops in winter even by one degree, the surface blood vessels will shut down and body will turn blue slowly, which is harmful for the inner organs to work. Hypothalamus gland then sends signals to adrenal glands and pituitary glands to make sure the liver releases more blood sugar as fuel for muscles, which are the main furnaces of the body, and on the other hand it starts dictating the body to shiver so that heat is produced by muscle activity.

Another important influence of hypothalamus gland can be witnessed while managing the water balance in the body. Our body contains 60% of water and every day we lose about one and a half litres of moisture via lungs, sweat and urine. If due to any reason it is lost more, one may die. This gland then balances all functions inside through pituitary gland and kidneys to absorb more water than usual and the urine becomes more concentrated and body feels thirsty to take more water, which maintains the water reservoir.

Behaviour of mind determines effect of medicines
Medicine is also on the one-way beginning to use the mind body connection for healing and defeating pain. By giving a placebo or dummy drug, 30% of patients will experience the same pain relief as if a real painkiller had been administered. The same dummy pill can be used to kill pain, stop excessive gastric secretions to ulcer patients; lower blood pressure or fight tumors. Even in cancer patients, there are numerous side effects of chemotherapy like loss of hair and nausea, and giving a sugar pill assuming that it is powerful anti-cancer drugs can give a lot of relief.

Angina pectoris, which is one of the heart diseases, causes typical squeezing and breathless pain. Cardiologist conclude that this pain occurs when at least one of the three coronary arteries is 50% block, a lesion on the inside of the arterial wall built up by dead cells, blood clots and fatty plaque. Let us compare two patients who are afflicted with this type of pain. One is fainted due to pain when one has only a single small lesion barely obstructing blood flow in one artery, while other is suffering massive, multiple blockage of upto 85% known to run races. It is, therefore, conclusive that the body is capable of producing any biochemical response once the mind has been given the appropriate suggestion.

Nervous system–body's software

The nervous system, which programmes the kind of messages being sent, functions as the body's software. The innumerable different hormones, neurotransmitters and other messenger molecules are the input being run through this software. All this constitutes the visible programming of your body, but the programmer is not visible. Thousands of decisions are being taken and countless choices made that enable your physiology in the mind-body system work every second.

Meditation is a supreme builder and service engineer of this so-called software nervous system and makes positive effects. It even slows or in some cases reverses the ageing process, as measured by various biological changes associated with growing old. It has been established that a long-term sincere meditator can reverse his biological age between 5 to 15 years and look younger than his chronological age. It is all-important to realise that you can reach a state during meditation, where communication with your mind and every cell is possible.

Influence of Meditation on Human Psychology

When an individual gets on to the route to self-understanding through meditation, his perspective of mental state altogether changes. Practising meditation regularly transforms his inner attitude towards self and his life. One becomes aware of himself who is he and what he wants and thus is able to satisfy his desires and gets the feelings of fulfillment.

Our suffering arises when we develop attachment to the processes. When a person starts meditating, he understands the impermanent nature of such processes and further realises that attachment, which brings in sufferings passes away. When anything occurs he does not react to it immediately, instead closely observes it with equanimity.

Meditation is a long task requiring continuous application. When a person starts meditating, he realises that benefits appear on every step along the way, but to attain them requires repeated efforts. By working patiently, persistently and continuously, a meditator advances towards the goal.

Although there are number of benefits attached to meditation and they have a tremendous impact on human psychology, you will yourself realise and experience it when you start practising this amazing technique. However, we can summarise them in the following points:

Emergence from sufferings
Sufferings begin because of one's own ignorance. In the darkness of such ignorance the mind reacts to everything as liking, disliking, craving, and aversion and creates sufferings and lays down a chain of events that will bring nothing but sufferings in future. Through meditation one can liberate from sufferings.

Awareness of impermanence
Attachment to impermanence, and illusion is beyond one's control brings most of the sufferings. Meditator realises that by the combination of mental and physical processes there is only illusion of ego to which one is devoted. Having surveyed body and mind to the deepest level, this reality becomes very clear that nothing is exempted from the law of impermanence.

Mental training
Meditation gives a sort of mental training that enables a person to observe himself consciously. As we take hygienic food to maintain physical strength, mental exercise also strengthens in the same manner. Through conscious learning to observe ourselves, we find balance of mind even in a difficult situation to review things with an objective mind and take positive and appropriate action.

Ego purification
On attaining materialistic achievements most of the time, mind keeps on reinforcing ego and one becomes much aware of his own

selfishness and egocentric self-love conditioning. As one practises meditation, he realises that even his love for others is his self-love only. If you love someone and are very attached to him, you naturally tend to build up high expectations from him. The moment he starts behaving differently, all your love is gone which indicate your intention to be self-loved only. An egoist person tends to belittle others, lower their importance and increase one's own image only.

But through meditation he can no longer hurt anyone or do anything that would hurt others. Meditation helps in liberating one from this harmful condition. One's ego is dissolved through meditation and one learns to develop real selfless love for others, without expecting anything in return.

Equanimity develops
When the mind is aware of equanimity, there is no reaction or cause to produce sufferings, hence one stops making sufferings. By developing equanimity, one tends to judge things and events with impartial and balanced mind without craving or aversion.

Efficient decision-making
If the mind is unbalanced, one is not able to take decisions efficiently and on the other hand with a calm and balanced mind, whatever decision one takes is effective, perfect and efficient. Clarity in decision-making, and high conviction on decision taken is achieved. Work efficiency increases as one gets focused and concentrated. His memory improves with mental alertness and mental ability also sharpened.

Development of goodwill towards others
Through meditation one understands that his own happiness cannot be obtained at the expense of others. Therefore having emerged from sufferings and liberation one seeks to share love and compassion with others. With the force or strength of pure and relaxed mind, one can easily create peaceful and harmonious atmosphere for the benefit of all.

Concentration
Success of world's famous personalities, whether in the field of art or science, lies in their focused and concentrated behaviour. It is very important to be aware of the benefits of the activities we perform. The immediate benefit of meditation is increased concentration

power, thereby increasing efficiency. Obviously the person if concentrated and focused is able to perform more efficiently than others.

Mental peace
The very important benefit of meditation is mental peace which is very significant in our life, for example, decisions made with calm and relaxed mind are far better and beneficial for us. Calm and relaxed people are in a better position to analyse and solve problems than people with agitated and confused mind. Mental peace decreases excitement and increases stability. It helps people remain stable even in difficult situations.

Mental peace and concentration are interdependent. Concentrated mind automatically achieves peace, while if the mind is not peaceful but agitated, one cannot concentrate. Presence of concentration in any field truly indicates the presence of peaceful mind.

Mental ability enhances
Our body and mind are connected with each other, so meditation affects the body as well as mind simultaneously. Meditation sooths and purifies one's mind to increases tolerance power. Mental activities like perception, sensation and receptiveness get sharpened.

The more we fill our mind with positive qualities, the less room is there for negative feelings to manifest. Hence, one reason we practise meditation is to train our mind to develop its pleasant qualities. There is, however, a more important and fundamental aim of meditation–to attain wisdom or enlightenment.

MEDITATION TECHNIQUES

There are numerous meditation techniques evolved throughout the world for the development of mankind and few of them are very simple and useful one as you go on practising. However few tips of each technique are briefed in the following chapters, but to get the best results of each one requires the following basic elements:
- Confidence, determined approach and non-discriminatory attitude towards meditation.
- A quiet, peaceful environment and a comfortable posture.
- Time to practise without interruption at a convenient and conducive time of the day. The best times are early in the morning and late at night
- A commitment to include daily meditation in your life as part of your daily routine.
- Understanding with patience that the results of meditation may not be experienced or even noticed for quite some time.

The various meditation techniques discussed in the following chapters are here under–

1. Vipassana Meditation
2. Chakra Meditation
3. Mantra Recitation
4. Pollution Free Meditation
5. Tranquil Meditation (Trataka)
6. Energy Healing Meditation
7. Ascension Meditation

8
Vipassana Meditation

Truly to come out of miseries

It is experienced that each and everyone says that he is having this or that problem in his day-to-day life and he always blames others for this. But the origin of suffering exists within us only, and it is very easy to come out of such sufferings and miseries. When we understand our own reality, we shall recognise the solution to the problem of suffering itself. Knowing our own nature, and ourselves we can solve all the problems of this materialistic world.

As a true belief we all have a physical aspect. This is the most apparent portion of us, readily perceived by all the senses. Superficially one can control the body, which moves and acts according to the conscious desire. But on other level, all the internal organs function beyond our control and without our will. At the very deeper level we know nothing of the incessant biochemical reactions occurring within each cell of the body. All such actions are carried out and controlled by our mind, which has two parts, viz., conscious and subconscious mind.

Along with the physical process there is a psychic process too. Although it cannot be touched or seen, it seems even more intimately connected with mind than our bodies. We can imagine a picture or a future existence without the body, but we cannot imagine any such existence without the mind. Yet how little we know about the mind and how little we are able to control it, and how often it refuses to do what we want, and does what we do not want.

Lord Buddha developed the vipassana meditation 2500 years ago towards liberalisation of oneself from miseries in a very simple way. *Pashayan* in Sanskrit means seeing and *Vipassana* means seeing true (as it is) within the body. This is a quite simple meditation technique just observing what is happening within the body. Human body is a composition of five elements; the world too is a formation of same elements. Hence by observing change within the body leads to understanding of the change due to contact of mind and metal (five elements) which is reoccurring in the outside world also. On the basis of impermanent nature of all beings, the equanimity develops keeping aside the craving and aversion.

Some people think that they are satisfied and happy with superficial pleasures of life, but they are ignorant of the agitation deep within their mind. They remain under the illusion that they are happy but their pleasures are not lasting. The tensions generated in the unconscious mind keeps on increasing; to appear sooner or later at the conscious level of mind and the so called happy people become miserable.

Since all the problems arise first in the mind, we must confront them at the mental level itself. To understand mind in a better way, we must first understand the processes attached to it.

For further process of establishing the overall relationship between the mind and body, the mind has four processes viz. (a) consciousness, (b) perception, (c) sensation and (d) reaction.

The first process, the consciousness is the receiving part of the mind, the act of undifferentiated awareness or cognition. It simply registers the occurrence of any phenomenon, the reception of any input, physical or mental. It notes the raw data of experience without assigning labels or making value judgements.

The second mental process is perception, the act of recognition. This part of the mind identifies whatever has been noted by the consciousness. It distinguishes, labels, and categorises the incoming raw data and makes evaluation. These evaluations can be positive or negative.

The next part of the mind is sensation. Actually as soon as any input is received, sensation arises, a signal flashes that something is happening. So long as the input is not evaluated, the sensation remains neutral. But once a value is attached to the incoming data, the sensation becomes pleasant or unpleasant depending on the evaluation given.

Finally, reaction the fourth part of mental functioning completes the process of actions both at the mental as well as at physical level. If the sensation is pleasant, a wish is formed to prolong and intensify the experience. If it is an unpleasant sensation, the wish is to stop it and to push it away. The mind reacts with liking or disliking. For example, when the ear is functioning normally and one hears a sound, cognition is at work. When the sound is recognised as words, with positive or negative connotation, perception has started functioning. Next sensation comes into play. If the words are of praise, a pleasant sensation arises, and if they are abusive, an unpleasant sensation arises. At once reaction takes place at body level. If the sensation is pleasant, one starts liking it, wanting more words of praise. If the sensation is unpleasant one starts disliking it and wants to stop the abuse, which is again apparent at body level.

The same steps occur whenever any of other senses receives an input, the mind starts at all four levels, consciousness, perception, sensation and reaction. Whenever if any input is repeated over a longer period of time and has taken a pronounced, intensified form, it is deeply superscripted at the base level of the subconscious mind. It then becomes a habit pattern, which may be positive or negative and becomes a part of our lifestyle.

All these reactions are like the lines drawn on the surface of a pool of water, as they are drawn they are erased. Others are like lines traced on sandy beach, if drawn in the morning they are gone by night, wiped away by the treads or the winds. The other are the lines cut deeply into rock with knife or hammer, they too will disappear as the rock erodes, but it will take ages for them to disappear and decide our behavioural pattern.

Throughout each day of our lives we keep generating reactions. All these reactions are defined as physical, vocal and mental. Normally we give more importance to physical reactions, less to vocal actions, and least to mental actions. Beating a person appears to us a graver action than speaking to him insultingly, and both seem more serious than an unexpressed ill-will towards the person.

But according to the law of nature, the mental action is most important. A physical or vocal action assumes totally different significance according to the intention with which it is done, for example, using a sharp edged razor used by a doctor and by a murderer. Physically their action is the same but at the mental level the surgeon acts out of compassion and the murderer out of hatredness.

Similarly in the case of speech, the intention is most important. Take an example of a man who quarrels and abuses other person calling him a fool and at the same time to call his child a fool who is playing in the mud where he speaks out of love. In both cases the words are same but express virtually opposite states of mind. So it is most important to understand that the words and deeds or their external effects are merely consequences of mental action. It is the only mental action, which is called karma, the cause of which will give results in future.

To analyse ourselves, at the end of each day we should try to remember the reactions; we shall be able to recall only one or two actions, which made a deep impression that day. We must further repeat this exercise at the end of a month and at the end of a year. Ultimately any deeper reactions which are deeply subscribed will play for our whole life. These are fruitful if positive and very dangerous if negative.

To come out of sufferings or sorrows, we must train our mind to register maximum positive actions for the overall behavioural development at all fronts because all such deep rooted actions further become our karma. We must include the following simplest exercise in our daily routine:

Vipassana Meditation–a Simple Exercise

- Choose a peaceful and non-disturbing place where you can sit for a longer time.
- Sit comfortably in a posture in which you can remain for a period of more than half an hour.
- Start observing your breath and concentrate on your nostrils, feeling the touch of incoming and outgoing breath continuously.
- Continue this exercise for at least three days till your mind is fully concentrated at one point.
- Start observing the sensations throughout your body from top of the head to the tip of your toes.
- While sitting in a posture constantly without changing for a longer period, you will experience different wanted or unwanted types of sensations.
- Practising continuously, you will observe that these sensations change at every moment. They are impermanent.
- Keep on observing these sensations by an objective mind not reacting at all and strengthening your equanimity by keeping away craving towards any favourable sensations and aversion towards any unfavourable sensations.

- This continued practice of equanimity would lead you to come out of miseries, understanding the impermanent nature of everything, which is applicable to the whole world and even the universe.
- In this way you will always feel happy, satisfied and tranquil.
- Your entire body as well as the whole atmosphere around you will be filled with positive vibrations.

During this state of tranquility, pray strongly for the well-being of each and everyone known or unknown, near or far away, living or non-living. May your positive vibrations spread towards the well-being of all.

9
Chakra Meditation

There are seven chakras located throughout the body, each has its own unique qualities and characteristics. These are considered to be the focal points of energy within our body.

These are located at important parts of the body from pelvic to head and are used to control the allocated organs within the area. Therefore, all the related organs are directly affected by the properties of that particular chakra.

Concentrating on a particular chakra activates its functioning properly to make flow of energy through connected organs assigned to the particular chakra. Following is an exercise to visualise each chakra and concentrate for energy creation for the wholesome development of body and mind.

Root Chakra
This chakra is located directly at the base of the spine, the centre of regeneration and reproductive organs. Its colour is red. It supports the ovaries and testes, prostate and spleen, one's health, constitution and security. In addition, it is focused on realisation of connectivity of the body to the material world.

Take a deep breath and loosen your body to the very base of your spine and locate the seat of first chakra. As you release the air, relax all the muscles in your toes, feet and legs. Take in more air and focus on your connecting point to the earth. Imagine that each breath you take activates and charges this energy chakra.

Naval Chakra

This chakra is located in the lower abdomen and associated with the acts of exchange of feelings of love, passion and sex. It has an orange colour. The feeling of pleasure is also linked with this chakra, so one may feel focused in this chakra during moments of harmony, generosity, group creativity, and selflessness.

Keeping the first chakra open, take a long deep breath in and lift your awareness from your root centre up to the second chakra. Here being the area of your sexual and reproductive organs allow the red energy to rush forward. Now let the air rush out and begin to consciously relax your genital muscles, buttocks, abdomen, hips, and pelvis keeping this chakra energised.

Solar Chakra

This chakra is located just above the navel and below the chest. Its colour is yellow. It is linked to your body's 'flight mechanism' and dynamics. This chakra is a focus point for your force and sense of transformation which works as a powerhouse of energy. The third chakra governs the pancreas, adrenal glands, organs of the stomach, intestines, kidneys, gall-bladder, and diaphragm.

This 'solar plexus' the energy centre controls breathing and digestion as oxygen and nutrients catalyse and release body heat. This centre is also called *hara*. It governs your gravitational force and is the source of personal power. Concentration and control of our personal energies originate from this point. One's sense of power and authority as well as self-control and discipline of the ego is controlled at this point.

Now take a deeper inhalation and lift your awareness to the third chakra, the solar plexus centre in your belly and keep it activated.

Heart Chakra

This chakra is located at the centre of the chest. Its colour is emerald green. It rules the heart, lungs, thymus, and adrenal glands. The native element is air and the feelings are light and expansive.

At the heart, your main motivator is the focus for love and understanding, harmony, peace, and cooperation. With an open heart, you learn the higher qualities of goodwill, devotion and sacrifice. This is the centre of the higher faculties of love, compassion, sympathy, forgiveness, and self-sacrifice. Here we become conscious participants in our own evolution. This centre is of pure unconditional love.

Take another slightly deeper inhalation and draw your attention up to the centre of your chest. As you exhale, settle your awareness on the heart centre and imagine feeling it stronger. Let each exhalation begin by relaxing you physically, and end by opening you spiritually like a flower unfolding its petals. Know yourself as a kind, generous, loving human being, worthy of giving and receiving the unconditional love that renews your soul. Pray for the welfare of all.

Throat Chakra

It is located in the throat area between one's chin and the top of the sternum. It has sky blue colour. This chakra is linked to one's power of communication. The throat chakra is the seat of personal creativity and self-healing. The thyroid is a master regulator of other endocrine glands and many of the body's complex metabolic systems and hormonal immune functions. Through this chakra one can realise truth and knowledge, honesty, kindness, and wisdom and how these elements can be conveyed through thoughtful speech.

Now inhale little forcefully and pull all the energy up from the deep red root centre, through all chakras in between to your throat area, which is a beautiful blue colour. Hold the air and energy for a moment while relaxing. Now relax and soften your tongue, vocal cords, neck muscles, shoulders, arms, and hands. With each exhalation, feel the radiant energy in your thyroid at the base of the neck.

Brow Chakra

This is a popular 'third eye' centre. The colour is indigo violet. It is located in the forehead, right above both the eyes. It is a tuning into your pineal gland, seated deep behind your eyes, just under the forebrain. It's like a tiny radio transmitter. Imagine that by settling into deep meditative perception, you can simply and easily turn on your higher functions like intuition, clairvoyance, telepathy, and precognition. Your third eye is like an x-ray laser beam probing the astral field and deeper soul levels of life, seeing the connecting patterns, the underlying universal energy and the meaning of things.

At this centre you have the potential to rise above to cosmic world. This chakra is related to perception beyond physical realm. One can also focus realisation of one's own soul, divine wisdom and peace of mind in this point.

With the throat chakra remaining open, take a deeper breath in and lift your awareness to the psychic centre between your eyebrows, in the middle of your forehead. Then relax deeply and imagine that each breath has the effect of opening this. You begin to perceive the divine connection.

Crown Chakra

It is like a thousand-petalled lotus opening upward at the top of your head. A pure and perfect, highly polished, rests in the centre of a beautiful and soft lotus flower in violet colour. The glands are the pituitary and thalamus, deep in the brain. It is located at the very top of the head.

This chakra is associated directly with dealings of the mind and spirit. Here is not something to attain but enlightenment. This chakra is deeply tied to the exploration of one's consciousness and place in space and time. Oneness with the universe, your spirit and will, inspiration, divine wisdom, all the things that deal with the higher self are rooted in this chakra. Here is the law of the universe to see beyond birth and death.

Breathe in and come up. Hold it and release concentrating at this chakra.

Now all your chakras are clean, charged and balanced. From the root to the violet/crown, all your chakras are spinning and whirling, full of energy and vitality. See the white energy that extends up and out from the crown chakra covering your whole body in an ocean of white energy. You are completely refreshed, calm and peaceful. Your energy is balanced and you are full of vitality.

10
Mantra Recitation

In Hindu mythology there is a strong belief that by chanting different mantras, works as remedial measures to dissolve the maleficent effects of planets' energies. For every planet different mantras are framed in our Shastras, the holy books,

Few of them are narrated below:

Mantras of Planets:

PLANET	MANTRA
SUN	ॐ घृणिः सूर्याय नमः।
MOON	ॐ सों सोमाय नमः।
MARS	ॐ अं अंगारकाय नमः।
MERCURY	ॐ बुं बुधाय नमः।
JUPITER	ॐ वृं वृहस्पतये नमः।
VENUS	ॐ शुं शुक्राय नमः।
SATURN	ॐ शं शनेश्चराय नमः।
RAHU	ॐ रां राहवे नमः।
KETU	ॐ कें केतवे नमः।

How Mantras Work

Every vibration has a corresponding sound and everything in the universe too has a vibration and thus a sound. Each atom, molecule, cell, object, group of objects, and even the entire universe has its own collection of vibrations and unique sounds.

When you chant a mantra, you merge with the sound vibration and become one with the energy wavelength of the object of your mantra. Mantra chanting makes you one with everyone, everywhere who is chanting that mantra and with everyone who has ever chanted the mantra.

By chanting a mantra, your cells, molecules, atoms, and subatomic particles all vibrate in the same wavelength as the mantra. Once attuned with this vibration you connect with everything resonating on that plane of existence. It's like tuning a radio.

'Om' Mantra Chanting

Chanting of 'Om' mantra in Hindu mythology is considered to be very pure and sacred.

Sanskrit Om

The meaning of 'Om'

Om is the universal sound. It is within every word and everything. When you chant 'Om', you merge with all energy and all forms, from the subatomic to the universal, from the most gross to the most divine. And when you are tuned perfectly, you will receive holy frequencies clearly and merge and emerge at one with the source of all and live happily.

Before the beginning, the Brahma (absolute reality) was one and non-dual. He thought, "I am only one — may I become many." This caused a vibration, which eventually became sound and this sound was 'Om'. Creation itself was set in motion by the vibration of 'Om'.

The closest approach to Brahma is that first sound, 'Om'. Thus, the sacred symbol of 'Om' has become emblematic of Brahma just as images are emblematic of material objects. The vibration produced by chanting 'Om' in the physical universe corresponds to the original vibration that first arose at the time of creation.

The 'Om' (AUM) is a widely recognised mantra and has a variety of meanings; one of its most significant uses is for meditation. Three sounds of AUM ("A", "U" and "M") symbolises specific states of consciousness. After these three parts of the 'Om' mantra, there is a silence.

The A is deep and comes from the throat. It is pronounced without any part of the tongue or palate in contact. The U sound comes from the middle of the sounding board, the palate. In Sanskrit, the A and U join together becomes O. The sound of O vibrates from the navel/solar plexus area and sent up to the sternum to the voice region, the lips, where the M sound is prolonged and vibrated up to the crown of the head.

This vibrating M is felt intellectually and metaphysically in every cell of the body and is beamed out lovingly, soothingly, powerfully to everything, everyone and everywhere. A stands for physical or material world perceptible to the senses, U represents the astral and dream planes. M is the unknown, deep sleep which contains the entire spectrum of sound, words, world, and concepts. So 'Om' represents the source of all light, love and wisdom.

It is advantageous for spiritual development to consider the theological, philosophical and mystical aspects of 'Om' while chanting with your physical eyes closed, looking through the third eye and paying attention to your breath. This may seem complex and complicated, but once it gets started, it happens naturally as 'Om' reveals itself to you.

The symbol 'Om'
Just as the sound of 'Om' represents the real state of Brahma, the symbol 'Om' written in Sanskrit also represents everything. The material world in waking state is symbolised by the large lower curve. The deep sleep state is represented by the upper left curve. The dream state, lying between the waking state below and the deep sleep state above, emanates from the confluence of the two.

The point and semicircle are separate from the rest and rule the whole world. The point represents the state of absolute consciousness. The open semicircle is symbolic of the infinite and the fact that the meaning of the point cannot be grasped if one limits oneself to finite thinking.

The power of chanting 'Om'
The chanting of 'Om' drives away all worldly thoughts and removes distraction and infuses new vigour in the body. Those who chant 'Om' definitely have a powerful, sweet voice. Whenever you take a stroll, you can chant 'Om'. You can also sing 'Om' in a beautiful way. The rhythmic pronunciation of 'Om' makes the mind serene and pointed, which infuses the spiritual qualifications and ensures self-realisation.

Meditation on 'Om'
- Retire to a quiet place, sit down in a comfortable posture, close your eyes and completely relax your muscles and nerves.
- Concentrate on the space between your eyebrows and silence the conscious mind.
- Breathe into the heart centre up to the crown while you breathe in. On exhaling take the energy of breath throughout

the body, grounding it through the feet into the earth. Do this for five minutes.
- Begin to repeat 'Om' mentally while associating the ideas of infinity, eternity and immortality etc. You must repeat 'Om' with the feeling that you are the infinite and all pervading. Mere repetition of 'Om' will not bring the desired result. Keep the meaning of 'Om' always in heart.
- Feel that you are the pure, perfect, all-knowing, eternal, free, Brahma. Feel that you are absolutely conscious, the infinite and unchanging existence. Every part of your body should powerfully vibrate with these ideas.
- Practise regularly and steadily with sincerity, faith, perseverance, and enthusiasm in the morning, midday, evening and whenever you get time.

11
Pollution Free Meditation

We are aware of four kinds of pollutions namely, land, air, water, and noise which are of major concern today. Apart from these there exists one more kind, which is also not less dangerous and harmful than these. That pollution exists within the human body itself and is known as mental pollution. This pollution when materialises within, takes form of various kinds of tensions. Five major elements that lead to mental pollution are:

- **Lack of knowledge:** It is the basic cause of various other commotions. All other commotions generate from this one only.
- **Ego:** As long as a person surrenders himself to the God; he is not touched by this commotion, or far away from this commotion. But as soon as he starts feeling proud of his achievements, he is captured by ego. This ego leads to various kind of destructions, the more sensitive ego is, the more dangerous it is.
- **Craving:** After consuming some happiness, one feels like craving to have more of it, which empowers him and it is a human tendency. This is the reason why craving is being put in the category of commotion.
- **Aversion:** When there is some obstruction in the way of craving or achieving happiness, this commotion originates. It comes out in the form of anger.
- **Death fear:** It means fear of death. Various other unreasonable phobias also come into this category.

From the above commotions, craving and aversion are commonly known as '*Rag* and *Dwesh*'. *Ra*g is considered as one of the very important commotions because all kind of grieves are generated due to that. On the other hand, significance of *dwesh* can be explained from the fact that it is also based on anger.

All these elements lead to mental pollution. Consequently, if a person is an introvert, he destroys himself internally by being tense all the time and if he is extrovert, he affects the society adversely.

How this Pollution can be Eliminated

Polluted mind cannot be cured by medicines. Mind is a collection of memories, thoughts; and because of this, it can be cured through thoughts only. If a mind is filled with unhealthy thoughts, it is bound to behave negatively. So in order to cure, it is necessary to spray fresh and healthy thoughts into it.

These healthy thoughts can be very easily produced through intellect and knowledge. The mere understanding of the fact that commotions are the major cause of all the problems urge us to take a bold step towards purification of an unhealthy mind. The best way for the process of purification of mind is meditation in the following manner:

- Sit in a comfortable position, either in a chair or on the floor, with your back and head straight.
- You can 'warm up' with a couple of deep breaths.
- Close your eyes. Breathe through your nose. Focus on your breath - cool air in, warm air out. If the mind wanders, gently bring it back to the breath. Start with 5-10 minute meditation and work your way up to half an hour.
- A variation that may make things a little easier at the beginning is to count your breaths. Count up to four and then repeat over and over. You can add an 'and' between counts to fill up the space between breaths. It goes like this: inhale (1) exhale (and) inhale (2) exhale (and) inhale and so on up to four.
- Affirm strongly–"I am the master of my life. I am an open channel of creative energy. I am naturally enlightened. Perfect wisdom is in my heart. I feel happy and blissful just being alive. I am open to receive all the blessings of this abundant universe."
- More affirm, "I have to love and be loved. I love doing work and I am nicely rewarded creatively and financially. I am now attracting towards love, satisfaction and happy relationships in my life. The more I love myself, the more love I have to give others."

12
Tranquil Meditation (*Trataka*)

Conscious living is a very useful way for handling day-to-day stress. But if meditation induced awareness is created, it explores the real secrets of life. Through tranquil meditation the concentration is focused at a particular point, which further expands the consciousness in a broader and wiser way.

This meditation has been systematised on two main principles viz. right concentration and right awareness.

1. **Right concentration–goal of tranquility:** The first part of this meditation can be focused on right concentration. In this process the meditator is required to focus his entire attention at a specific object and become increasingly concentrated on it. Through this exercise the mind slowly withdraws from all external and internal stimuli and then leads to a state of pure and undistracted consciousness. The term 'tranquility' refers to the calming of mental processes, which results from this withdrawal.
2. **Right awareness–the goal of insight:** In order to achieve full liberalisation and enlightenment, meditator considers the logical state and the mental objects insight into the working of one's mind. The meditator becomes a detached observer of these objects of contemplation with the aim of achieving total and immediate awareness or mindfulness of all phenomena and due to this reason it has also been called 'mindfulness' meditation.

Preparation for Tranquil Meditation

It is advisable to practise this meditation in quiet and comfortable surroundings. Loose and comfortable dress is recommended during practise. To start with prepare yourself with the following material:

- Cut a white paper in 12 inches circle diameter with a black small pinpoint in the middle.

- Take another black paper in square dimension of 2' x 2'. Paste this white circle in the centre. This will make the circle more prominent for easy focusing on a small point.
- This object should be placed at eye level when viewed from a sitting position at a distance of 3 to 4 feet.
- Focus your eyes on the black point in the middle in a normal manner. If the eyes are wide open, they will become fatigued and if they are open too little, the mind will become drowsy. Both results will adversely affect the meditation. Do not become distracted by closely examining or analysing the object.
- Then alternatively open and close the eyes. While closing the eyes, try to perceive the picture of the object as if the eyes were open. Does not matter even if there is no perception.
- Slowly, slowly your eyes will automatically get closed comfortably and soothingly.
- In a shorter span of time you will attain the complete restful posture of the body all by itself effortlessly. This will keep your mind calm and concentrated peacefully and tranquilly.
- This moment will withdraw your mind from all external and internal stimuli and leading to a state of pure and undistracted consciousness. Although there may be number of thoughts coming and going into the mind, but the meditator becomes the sole observer of all.
- Reaching at this stage, a person becomes a detached observer of these objects of contemplation with the aim of achieving total and immediate awareness or mindfulness.
- During this stage of undistracted consciousness, observe all thoughts and contemplation and keep your mind in a state of deep tranquillity. As the moments of this tranquillity increase, the way of living altogether changes.
- This meditation should be practised daily at least for 5 minutes at the initial stage every day and increase it upto half an hour.
- Do not worry if during meditation, you face some obstacles like dissatisfaction, a wandering mind or drowsiness.

13
Energy Healing Meditation

As the name suggests, this meditation helps in healing by evoking universal cosmic energy. In this simple healing meditation, you send the powerful healing life force energy directly to the area it requires inside the body. This life force is the energy behind all healing. Wherever this energy is flowing in balance, there is perfect health and well-being. Wherever this energy is blocked or out of balance, illness manifests.

Practise this technique in the following manner:
- Sit in a comfortable position, either in a chair or on the floor, with your back and head straight.
- Take few deep breaths.
- As you inhale, feel yourself breathing the healing life force in through your solar plexus. Picture this life force as a very refined and light energy.
- As you exhale, gently direct this light energy to flow to the afflicted area taking out the blockages and ailments. If there is not a specific ailing area, disperse this light energy throughout your body as you exhale.
- Continue until you feel the area has received enough life force or otherwise practise at least for half an hour daily.

14
Ascension Meditation

Spiritual traditional masters have spoken of the ultimate goal of meditation and have called it as enlightenment; self-realisation, god realisation; cosmic consciousness or mukti etc. Currently, the term 'Ascension' is emerging in our collective consciousness to refer to this goal, so we use that term for consistency.

There are four basic principles which the heart and mind should follow:
1. Kindness towards all beings.
2. Compassion towards those who are suffering.
3. Sympathetic joy towards others.
4. Equanimity towards friends and foes.

This meditation is designed to stimulate the experience of ascension. It makes use of creative visualisation and imagination in the following way:
- Sit comfortably and reasonably straight.
- Concentrate on your breathing for few minutes till your entire body is relaxed completely.
- Visualise your higher self as a human-sized form of brilliant golden-white light just over your head.
- Imagine yourself slowly rising to merge with the light of your higher self. Your entire being is transformed to brilliant golden-white light.
- Visualise your surroundings becoming brighter and brighter, until there is nothing but a sea of golden white light, an ocean of spirit.
- Imagine your consciousness is expanding and you are merging with this ocean of cosmic light. Remain immersed in the ocean of light and pray for kindness towards all beings, compassion towards those who are suffering, sympathetic joy towards others and equanimity toward friends and foes, until you come out of meditation.